A PRIMER OF PSYCHOBIOLOGY

A Series of Books in Psychology

Editors

Richard C. Atkinson
Jonathan Freedman
Gardner Lindzey
Richard F. Thompson

A PRIMER OF PSYCHOBIOLOGY

BRAIN AND BEHAVIOR

Timothy J. Teyler
Harvard University

W. H. Freeman and Company
San Francisco

Library of Congress Cataloging in Publication Data

Teyler, Timothy J
    A primer of psychobiology.

    Includes bibliographical references and index.
    1.   Psychobiology.   I.   Title.   [DNLM:
1.   Behavior.   2.   Psychophysiology.   WL102 T356p]
QP360.T45   612'.82   74-20989
ISBN 0-7167-0749-7   3. Psychology, Physiological
ISBN 0-7167-0748-9 pbk.

9 8 7 6 5 4 3 2 1

to Lisbeth

CONTENTS

PREFACE

This is a book about the brain and behavior. The brain is a most fascinating organ, and I enjoy sharing with others the excitement I feel when considering its intricacies. Indeed, I hope others will enjoy reading this book as much as I enjoyed writing it.

A Primer of Psychobiology grew out of an introductory course in psychobiology that I taught at the University of California, Irvine. The course was designed for and limited to nonbiology majors. Thus, I faced the job of telling dance majors, English majors, and physics majors about the brain and behavior. For this reason, the book presupposes little or no specialized knowledge on the part of the reader.

Because I was writing for nonbiologists and for those in the early stages of psychological or biological education, I tried to keep jargon and specialized terminology to a minimum and to present readable, enjoyable, and informative text with a clear elaboration of concepts.

I wish to thank the people who assisted me in the preparation of this book. I am especially grateful to Nancy Kyle, Cheryl Real, and Donna Lloyd for their typing and retyping of my scribbled notes. Although the final result is my responsibility alone, I thank Richard F. Thompson, and Richard A. Roemer for their help, encouragement, and comment. I also thank the authors and the publishers who permitted the reproduction of their material.

Most of all I thank my wife and my child who put up with my absence during the many hours that I spent preparing this book.

Timothy J. Teyler
March 1974

Introduction

BRAIN BIOLOGY AND THE FUTURE OF MAN

A common theme running through media, advertisements, and political announcements is the deterioration of our environment and the need to do something about it. Almost everyone knows the causes of pollution and most know the means to a solution. Yet, given this knowledge man has been reluctant to act in a decisive manner. Some, of course, label those concerned about the environment as alarmists. Most people, however, see the continued degradation of this planet as a very serious threat to the future of life as we know it. Some perspective can be gained by using the analogy of a host–parasite relationship. The parasite depends upon the host for its existence. In a classical host–parasite relationship the balance between host and parasite is a critical one. If a parasite population increases, perhaps because of the health or numerousness of the host, the drain upon the resources also increases and the host population is weakened until it cannot support the parasite population. The host may be destroyed, thus destroying the parasite, or sufficient numbers of the parasite may abandon the host to allow recovery and perhaps a new resurgence of parasite population.

The common flea and the house cat provide an example of such relationships. If the flea is smart it will keep its numbers low enough that the cat is not overly damaged by flea bites and the consequences thereof. However, given a healthy cat (without a flea collar), the average flea generally does not display prodigious intellect but rather increases its numbers until the cat reacts adversely. As the infestation increases the animal will gradually weaken, thus becoming a less desirable host. At this point the high-IQ flea will "abandon ship" and set out for better territories. If the flea infestation continues unabated the poor cat will sink lower and lower and ultimately cease to provide *any* kind of habitat for the flea. Thus, the dumb flea fixes his own fate through flamboyant fecundity!

Man is the flea and the earth is the cat. To supply its biological and social demands, the burgeoning human population is putting a severe strain upon the planet's resources. Non-replaceable resources such as coal and oil are gradually being exhausted and renewable resources such as air and water are progressively being degraded. Much of modern man's impact on the earth is the result either of releasing into the environment vast quantities of nondegradable man-made products or of overloading existing biological purification systems. In efforts to remedy this situation, which to the Martian observer might look like a studied attempt to destroy his own niche, man is ominously inactive.

One reaction is that we need to understand man better in order to explain and perhaps ultimately control his behavior. The traditional disciplines dealing with the study of man have not been notably successful in understanding him. Perhaps it is too much even to suggest that the brain sciences can play a role in this historical quest. But by understanding the function of the central nervous system, we in effect understand man. Perhaps brain biology *is* the key to a future utopia. Or, like most things of great promise, a potential for misuse exists that might lead to an Orwellian nightmare.

This is a book about the brain; more than that, it is a book about what the brain does. The study of the brain as an organ of the body is generally carried out by neurophysiologists and anatomists. The study of what the brain does, that is, the behavior it produces is generally done by psychologists, sociologists, and the like. This book is a survey of a new field, *psychobiology*, which is a merging of the brain sciences and the behavioral sciences. Both psychobiology and this book represent an attempt to understand the *brain and behavior*.

The aim of this book is to examine briefly the kinds of behavior organisms are capable of producing. Some behaviors are very rudimentary and uninteresting. Other behaviors are the result of long years of learning. Still other behaviors come to us without any learning at all.

In this book we will look at (1) the nerve and brain cells, which are called neurons, that compose the brain, (2) the functional divisions of the brain, and (3) what happens when brain tissue is experimentally stimulated. The material covered in this book progresses from the most elementary to the most complex. The brain is considered first as an assemblage of neurons, and then as groups of neurons that share a common job, and finally as entire behavioral or motivational systems. The last chapter of the book, "Brain and Behavior," will examine several recent topics in the neurosciences that have captured the imagination of scientists and laymen alike. We will briefly examine the nature–nurture question, and find that the question itself is wanting. We will examine the "science-fiction" world of brain stimulation in man and in animals. And we will look at some recent work with a dramatic surgical approach that has given us much understanding concerning the operation of the cortex of the brain.

Throughout this book various terms appear in boldface type. These terms are defined and listed in a glossary at the end of the book.

Although the reader of this book will not emerge as a neuroscientist, it is my hope that he or she will emerge with a somewhat more clear understanding of basic brain functioning and how his or her daily behavior is controlled in its every expression by the interactions of brain cells.

A PRIMER OF PSYCHOBIOLOGY

1
LIFE IS BEHAVIOR

INNATE BEHAVIOR

From the protozoan, which lives as a single cell, to the incredibly complex human, with trillions of cells, one feature is common to all animal life—*behavior*. All forms of animal life behave with a bewildering diversity of expressions. The behavior of some organisms, such as the amoeba, is rather limited and unexciting, except perhaps to another amoeba. Other animals display complicated and intricate behaviors that often defy description and understanding. The behavior of man is the most complex and difficult to understand.

In an attempt to understand an organism we must then understand its behavior and the biological bases of that behavior. The perceptive reader will recognize that this approach to the study of man, the ultimate goal, is that of a **reductionist**. A reductionist seeks to explain a phenomenon by reducing it to the parts that make up the whole. The biological bases of behavior can be reduced to muscle movements and glandular secretions, which are generally the result of neural activity, which in turn is the result of chemical activity. Chemical activity can be understood in terms of changing molecular configurations, which can be formulated as precise relationships of particular atoms connected at certain submolecular bond angles and can be expressed by mathematical statements. The logical extension of reductionism is the expression of human behavior in mathematical terms. Admittedly we are quite far from the day when this will be done.

A first question to ask in understanding an organism is "What does it do?" Scientists have devised a scheme for ranking behaviors from the simplest to the most complex. Table 1 lists these behaviors in order of increasing complexity. Taxes and reflexes are both simple behaviors, ones compatible with the absence of awareness. A **taxis** is a movement toward or away from a stimulus. A moth's flying toward the light is a phototaxis, for example. A **reflex** is a protective reaction of

Table 1 Types of behaviors categorized in terms of primarily innate and primarily acquired behaviors. Within each category behaviors are listed in order of increasing complexity

Primarily Innate	Example
Taxes	Moth's moving toward light
Reflexes	Person's jerking hand from hot stove
Innate behavior sequences	Fighting of tropical fish

Primarily Acquired	Example
Behavior established by classical conditioning	Dog's salivating to a signal associated with food
Behavior established by instrumental conditioning	Cat's pressing a pedal to avoid a mild shock
Manipulation of symbolic elements	Your reading or writing

an organism and is generally a movement away from a potentially harmful stimulus. Examples of reflexes include coughing, sneezing, eye blinks, and limb withdrawal.

An **innate behavior sequence**, a considerably more complex behavior than a taxis or a reflex, is a complex sequence of unlearned behaviors elicited by a specific stimulus. To the casual observer innate behavioral sequences may look rather purposeful and well thought-out. Consider the fighting behavior of the stickleback, a commonly studied fish. If a male stickleback spies another male near his territory who is displaying a bright red belly—a sure sign of belligerence—he will attack the aggressive intruder. A man might stand in awe of this little fish, admiring his tenacity in defending his small part of the world against an intruder. A romantic observer, however, would be disappointed to learn that the fish will attack virtually anything possessing a red "belly"—including wooden models scarcely resembling fish—in the same manner. It seems that the stickleback is responding in a fixed way (by an aggressive behavior sequence) to a particular stimulus (the red belly) and that both the response and the stimulus are determined by the genetic inheritance the fish received at birth. That is, a stickleback reared in total isolation from all other living things would react in the same way to either an intruding red-bellied fish or a red-bellied model, thus eliminating the possibility that the behavior was learned (Fig. 1).

A similar story concerns the mating activities of a species of wasp. Upon meeting a receptive female the male proceeds with a courtship dance and the subsequent copulation. Again, a romantic observer would be disturbed to view the male wasp addressing the motions of the courtship dance and copulation to a piece of paper on which are spread the squashed remains of a female. In this case the effective stimulus, known as the **releaser**, which elicits the stereotyped response is the odor of the female—and this odor, in any context, is sufficient to release the male's mating behavior. Do not get the idea that mother nature is playing a haphazard game—for a stickleback is rarely confronted with a red-bellied wooden model in

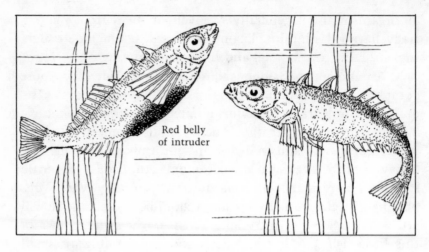

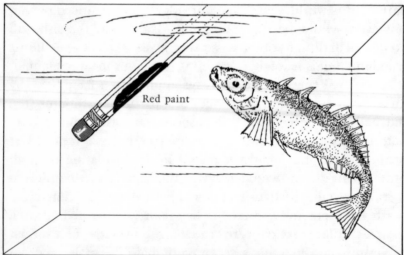

Figure 1 Species-specific aggressive behavior in the stickleback. The male fish will attack an "invading" fish displaying a red belly. Similarly, the fish will attack an object as remote from a fish as a pencil, provided that the pencil has red paint on its "belly."

nature, just as the male wasp rarely encounters the squashed remains of a female. Because of this, the innate behavior sequences are effective devices controlling the behavior of an organism.

Taxes, reflexes, and innate behavior sequences—are primarily unlearned. The behaviors do not develop as a result of practice or teaching—they are inborn. The mechanisms of their actions remain quite mysterious, but it is known that the genetic inheritance that every living thing receives from its parents contains coded information regarding behavior sequences just as surely as it contains a blueprint for the anatomy of the organism. One of the great challenges facing biology is in the unraveling of the "genetic code." Once the mechanism by which information is passed on from generation to generation is understood, mankind will have at his fingertips the potential to eradicate many of the diseases plaguing man today, as there is a sizable genetic component in many of them. He will have the potential for correcting genetic accidents like mental retardation and deformities. He will also have the potential to modify the genetic code and so modify man himself.

This is not merely a dream or a nightmare but the form that reality is rapidly assuming. It is only a matter of time until some, if not all, of these possibilities are realities. The potential to change man is an awesome power—one that could benefit man greatly or could destroy him. The potential for good or harm far surpasses that of nuclear energy, with more profound effects. Biologists of the present and future are in the same position physicists found themselves in during the 1940's. The physicists were working on an awesome source of power—nuclear fission, which could be harnessed for the furtherance or hindrance of mankind. Some physicists today, as then, feel that the military applications of nuclear energy are wrong and that as scientists they failed in their responsibility to mankind in allowing their discoveries to be used in such a manner. Whether they are right or wrong only history can judge. The point is that biologists are now on the verge of uncovering an even more awesome power. The responsibility for the wise use of this power rests on all of us as it will affect all of society.

Fortunately for life on earth biologists are well aware of the awesome potential of their work. In July of 1974 a group of prominent biologists, including Harvard's Nobel laureate James D. Watson, called for a temporary ban on certain experiments dealing with the genetic manipulation of living cells and viruses. This appeal for a worldwide moratorium on research by scientists active in the area was instigated by the discovery of enzymes capable of inserting "foreign" genes into living cells. The scientists were concerned about the possibility that such "new" organisms might escape and infect the population—which would have no resistance to the organisms! The possibility of such an occurrence was the theme of Michael Crichton's science fiction (or fact?) book *The Andromeda Strain*.

In this section we have seen that behaviors can be ranked from simple to complex. We have also seen that some behaviors are innate, that is, they are present as a result of genetic inheritance. Most of the innate behaviors in man are relatively uninteresting but important reflexes. We have seen how some behaviors can be quite precise and elaborate even though they are entirely innate. The expression of innate behaviors is not entirely without environmental influence. Every organism interacts with his environment. This interaction of genetic inheritance and environment determines the final behavioral outcome.

LEARNED BEHAVIOR

The behaviors to be discussed below have one point in common—all are learned or acquired, none are inherited per se. A moment's reflection will bring the realization that an acquired behavior could not exist in the absence of an organism, and that organisms are built according to an innate genetic blueprint. It is futile to attempt to separate out a behavior as "purely acquired" because an innate framework is needed for the expression of the acquired behavior. The behaviors discussed below utilize an innate framework, but the specific response to the environment situation is *not* "built into" the organism.

Habituation and Sensitization

Habituation is the reduction of a preexisting response. An example should serve to clarify the meaning of habituation. A sudden noise causes us to direct our attention to the source. If the noise is repeated, we may in time no longer respond to it—we have then habituated. The opposite of habituation, **sensitization**, produces an augmented response to a stimulus. You may at some time have been sitting in a movie theater engrossed in a suspense film, such as Alfred Hitchcock's *Psycho*, when someone behind you suddenly sneezed causing you to jump out of your chair. That was a sensitized response. Normally the sound of an unexpected sneeze would be barely attended to, but the level of arousal may be so heightened by a frightening movie that virtually any stimulus will elicit a vigorous response. The two processes of habituation and sensitization appear to be basic to all species. Nerve cells exhibiting the properties of habituation, sensitization, or a combination of the two have recently been discovered in the spinal cord of the cat. Habituation and sensitization are particularly clear examples of the interaction between nature and nurture. The existing response (provided by nature) is changed as a result of the organism's interaction with the environment (nurture).

Classical Conditioning

Classical conditioning (also called associative conditioning) was discovered by the Russian scientist I. P. Pavlov. Pavlov, a physiologist at the beginning of his career, was studying the chemical composition of salivary fluid. To collect saliva

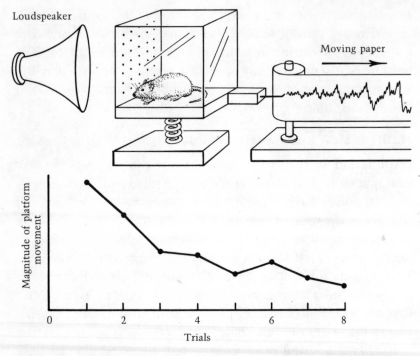

Loudspeaker

Moving paper

Magnitude of platform movement

Trials

Figure 2 Habituation of startle response in the rat. The rat is suspended on a spring-mounted platform. Periodically a loud tone is transmitted through the loudspeaker and this causes the animal to jump. The jumps are recorded on moving paper, and it is found that their magnitude decreases with repetition of the stimulus. Below is plotted the magnitude of the platform movement versus repeated trials.

for analysis, he first placed a tiny tube into the salivary ducts of dogs. Then meat powder was squirted into the mouths of the dogs whereupon they salivated. Pavlov's discovery hinged on the accidental observation that after the procedure had been repeated several times the dogs began to salivate when the assistant who had given them the meat powder on earlier occasions entered the room—*before he squirted meat powder into their mouths*! The dogs had apparently learned to associate the sight of the assistant with the receipt of meat powder and therefore salivated in anticipation at the sight of him. Thus, conditioning is the establishment of a new response where one did not exist previously. Pavlov abandoned his work on the composition of salivary fluids and immediately began to devise experiments to follow up this observation. He and his students studied many aspects of classical conditioned behavior—such studies continue even to this day.

It is now known that most simple behaviors can be conditioned. The procedure is to associate repeatedly a neutral signal (ringing of a bell, flashing of a light) closely in time with a meaningful stimulus (electric shock, puff of air directed toward the eye, presence of food). The neutral signal will, after a number of pairings, elicit the response that originally only the meaningful stimulus elicited. For example, a rat will normally not respond strongly to a brief tone. It does, however, respond to an electric shock applied to its feet. It responds in a great many ways: by squealing, jumping, gnawing, urinating, defecating, changing respiration rate and heart rate, and so forth. If a light is turned on just before the application of a shock to the rat, the light alone, after a number of pairings, will elicit some of the responses. Such **conditioned responses** are learned and may disappear if the meaningful stimulus is omitted for a period of time (Fig. 3).

People have conditioned such responses as heart rate, skin resistance, and eye blinks. The Russians have reported conditioning a wide variety of responses, including such improbable ones as blood sugar level, intestinal contractions, and gall bladder twitches! Classical conditioning is thought to bring about an elementary kind of learned behavioral change exceeded in simplicity only by habituation and sensitization. Such learned behavioral changes are possible because of **behavioral plasticity**.

Instrumental Learning

By way of introduction it should be pointed out that Harvard's B. F. Skinner deserves the credit for the upsurge of interest in instrumental conditioning in the United States. Most of the

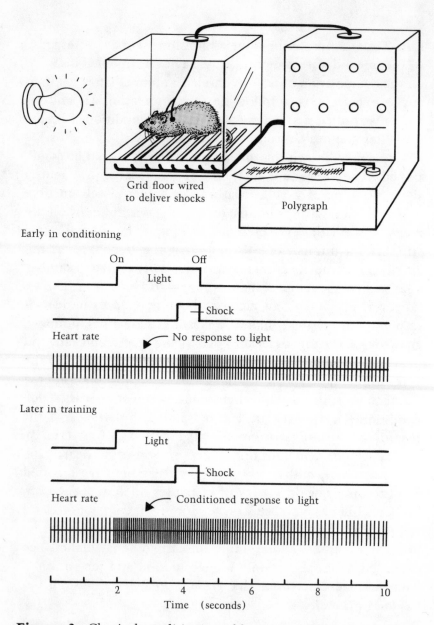

Grid floor wired
to deliver shocks

Polygraph

Early in conditioning

On   Off

Light

Shock

Heart rate   No response to light

Later in training

Light

Shock

Heart rate   Conditioned response to light

2   4   6   8   10
Time   (seconds)

Figure 3 Classical conditioning of heart rate in the rat. Electrodes detect the heart rate of the rat, which is then displayed on a polygraph. Early in conditioning the light, which flashes on just before an electric shock is delivered, fails to elicit any change in the animal's heart rate. Later in training the animal's heart rate increases dramatically each time the light goes on, before the shock is received.

behavior that humans engage in daily can be considered as instrumental learning or manipulation of symbolic elements. Through classical conditioning an organism does nothing to *alter* the course of events. The saliva, for example, does not prevent or augment the delivery of the meat powder. Through **instrumental learning**, however, an organism has the capability of controlling an external event by its own behavior. Consider the task of training a dog to roll over. It would be convenient to present a stimulus to which the dog would respond by rolling over. This stimulus could be associated with the command "roll over." This, as you can see, is classical conditioning. Unfortunately, we cannot find such a stimulus. Well then, how do people train dogs to roll over? They get the dog to roll over (or something approaching it) and then praise him or give him a treat. In other words, instead of producing the desired behavior by a stimulus they "get the dog to do it" by any of a number of ways, and *then reinforce the action*. Operationally, we can say that the "**reinforcer** tends to increase the probability of repetition of the response preceding it." Somewhat anthropomorphically, we can say that the animal perceives the reinforcer as desirable and attempts to provoke its reappearance by doing what it had done immediately prior to past reinforcements.

A favorite student laboratory project is to train rats or pigeons to "dance" by using instrumental conditioning. A hungry animal is placed in a testing chamber equipped with a response lever or button and a food dispenser. The "dance" is a rather simple one—going around in a complete circle. The student reinforces the animal (by giving it food) every time it makes a movement in the "correct" direction. Eventually the animal makes a complete circle. Some animals learn the "dance" quite well and will continue to perform until no longer hungry. The effect of reinforcement can be quite perplexing if the observer is unfamiliar with the preceding events. Food was delivered automatically to some pigeons in a cage at periodic intervals and without regard to their behavior. When observed after a time some of the birds were behaving in what seemed a strange manner. Some were flapping their wings, others were moving about, some were pecking furiously, some remained in one corner of the cage. It seems that the animals had been reinforced for what they happened to be doing at the time of food delivery. Little did the birds know that their behavior had nothing to do with the delivery of food. They were behaving superstitiously. We may wonder how many of man's behaviors are based similarly upon coincidental reinforcements.

Animals can be taught to do a great variety of tasks by using instrumental reinforcements. A rat can learn to press a bar in order to obtain food. A monkey can be taught to push a button to obtain a brief view of other monkeys at play. Animals can also learn to respond in order to *prevent* the delivery of an electric shock. Animals can learn to be quite discriminating about a particular stimulus. A pigeon placed in a "Skinner box" equipped with red and blue lights provides an example. Pecks on a button when the red light is on will result in food being made available to the bird. A peck on the same button when the blue light is on will turn off all the lights in the box, an unpleasant state of affairs as far as the bird is concerned. Placed in such a box, a pigeon quickly learns to peck when the red light is on and to refrain from pecking when the blue light is on. The behavior of the bird is under the control of the colored lights (Fig. 4).

The behavior of man is similarly under the control of external stimuli associated with positive and negative reinforcers. Most of us refrain from swearing in front of our grandparents and wear casual clothing on picnics. Our behavior is thus controlled somewhat by the external stimuli provided by grandparents and picnics. These stimuli have gained the power of controlling our behavior through previous exposure to positive and negative reinforcements associated with them. This is not to say that a reinforcement need occur every time. A gambler does not stop gambling because he fails to win on each throw of the dice. A motorist does not continually go

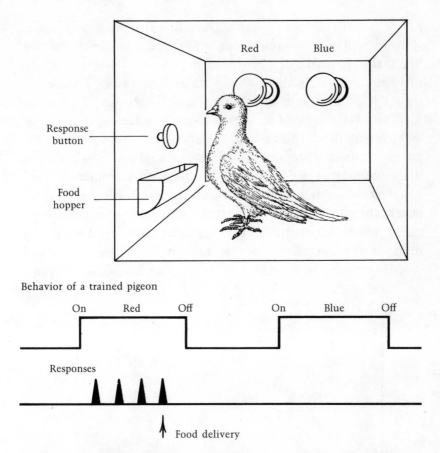

Figure 4 Instrumental conditioning of the pigeon. The pigeon is in a Skinner box equipped with a red and a blue light. The animal can peck at the response button in order to obtain food. When the red light is on, food delivery follows four pecks at the response button. A peck when the blue light is on turns off all the lights in the chamber—a situation that the pigeon finds aversive. Below is shown the record of pecking behavior of a trained pigeon.

through red traffic lights even though he realizes that he will not be caught every time. Our behavior is controlled effectively by occasional reinforcements. The same is true of animals in a Skinner box working for a food reward. They can be trained to respond at a high level for infrequent or partial reinforcements.

It is difficult, if not impossible, for the average American student willfully to stop or slow his heart. It is equally unlikely that he can alter the blood flow in his left ear. Yet rats can be taught to do these feats with apparent ease. Two scientists, N. Miller and L. DiCara, have succeeded in instrumentally training rats to increase or decrease heart rate and local blood flow. Miller and DiCara have also succeeded in training rats to decrease blood pressure and are now applying their techniques to humans afflicted with chronically high blood pressure. If successful, the treatment holds the promise of lengthening life and alleviating the misery associated with many kinds of cardiovascular diseases (Fig. 5). Procedures such as these utilize what is known as **biofeedback**—the "feeding back" or informing a subject of a biological event.

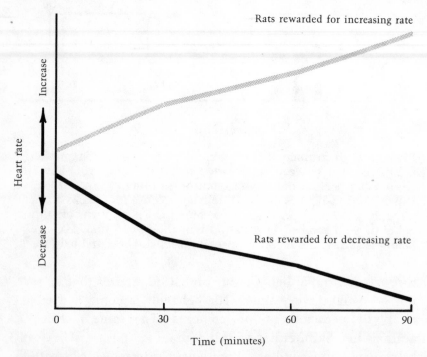

Figure 5 Instrumental conditioning of heart rate in rats. Rats were rewarded with electrical brain stimulation for either increasing or decreasing their heart rate.

It is often possible to alter a biological response by means of instrumental reinforcements. Biofeedback can be used to modify virtually any biological event—including physiological events within a person of which he is normally unaware—and has been most used medically in connection with blood pressure, heart rate, and brain activity. Especially with brain activity, there are psychological changes that accompany the biological changes.

For many years psychologists had held that such autonomic nervous system responses as heart rate and blood pressure were not susceptible to change by instrumental conditioning procedures. Casual knowledge tends to support such a view. After all, how many of us know persons who can alter their heart rate or blood pressure? The experiments of Miller and DiCara are at odds with casual knowledge in indicating that such training is possible. Furthermore, persons from cultures other than our own *are* capable of altering these bodily functions. Indian mystics and others can actually slow their heart rate and stick pins through their skin without bleeding (an example of local control of blood flow). People raised in the "outward" oriented Western cultures are amazed and disbelieve these feats, claiming them to be hoaxes. In fact, Eastern cultures emphasize a more "inward" orientation. An orientation that makes these feats possible.

In a standard instrumental conditioning situation an animal may, by responding, bring forth a desirable, or positive, reinforcer or avoid an undesirable, or negative, reinforcer. The organism thus has some control over its environment. Our daily activities are usually organized or structured as much as possible to maximize positive reinforcement and minimize negative reinforcement—all by adjustment of our behavioral responses to the environment.

Manipulation of Symbolic Elements

The most complex behavior we engage in is the **manipulation of symbolic elements**: that is, communication via symbols that have a common meaning, for example, language. Herein man is unique, far surpassing the ability for communication exhibited by any other animal species. Learning and using a language entails not only the acquisition of a vocabulary but the learning of a set of rules governing the use of words. We know that skills in manipulating symbols (speaking, writing, problem solving) differ widely from person to person, but we do not know the reason why. We know that with training people can improve their ability to manipulate symbols, but we are not sure how their learning is achieved. Clearly, we have barely begun to understand the complexities of human behavior.

Learned behaviors, like innate behaviors, can be classified from simple to complex. One of the simpler of learned behaviors is habituation, which is not the establishment of a new response, but the reduction of an existing response. The converse of habituation is sensitization, or the increase of a response. Laboratory models of learning include associative conditioning and instrumental learning. Associative conditioning, discovered by Pavlov, depends upon the association of two events in time: the man or animal can do nothing about the events, but simply learns to respond to them. In instrumental learning, on the other hand, the individual's behavior is "instrumental" in bringing about a reinforcement. Instrumental conditioning was given its greatest impetus in the United States by B. F. Skinner. Instrumental conditioning is somewhat more complex than associative conditioning in that the individual's options are much greater, and its freedom to respond in order to obtain a reinforcement or to avoid one is much greater. The behavior of man is under the control of stimuli delivered on partial reinforcement schedules, and these occasional reinforcements are effective in controlling our behavior. Instrumental conditioning techniques have been applied toward changing cardiovascular function in rats and even in man. The most complex behavior that humans engage in is the manipulation of symbolic elements. By this is meant language, calculation, and abstract thought. Man alone is capable of achieving great feats in terms of manipulation of symbolic elements. This is what makes man the most interesting and ascendant of species. Our knowledge of brain mechanisms of this ability is rudimentary.

THE STUDY OF BEHAVIOR

The study of behavior can proceed in many contexts. We unknowingly study behavior every day of our lives when we interact with other people and animals and make judgments about their personalities, intelligence, and how we should react with them. Admittedly, this is not a very scientific study of behavior. We are influenced by a good many biases, myths, and prejudices that affect our judgments. The scientific study of behavior attempts to eliminate these influences that taint our judgments. This is difficult as scientists are eminently human and carry with them as many biases as do other men. How, then, do they manage to keep these biases from clouding their judgments?

A scientist, when observing a behavior, attempts to specify as precisely as possible the phenomenon he sees. As measuring instruments are free of human biases, the scientist, whenever he can, will use an instrument to record and describe behavior. This implies that the instrument is accurate and that it actually measures what it is purported to. Examples of instruments used in the measurement of behavior range from a simple stop watch to a large computer.

In addition to specifying the response of the organism in precise terms, the scientist must also describe exactly what gave rise to the response. This is also rather difficult because many behaviors of an organism are dependent upon the sum total of experiences preceding the event at hand. Merely explaining the features of a task that an organism is currently facing is often not sufficient because it does not take into account the experiences the organism has had in similar situations in the past—experiences that no doubt affect the behavior of the organism. The solution is to limit the experiences encountered by the organism under test. One reason for using laboratory animals is thus clear: we can specify the experiences they have had because we have controlled their environment throughout their lives. By choosing highly inbred animals we can also ensure that there will be little genetic difference between such organisms. Obviously, we cannot be so rigorous for human subjects, or for that matter, for many animals that have not been reared as laboratory animals. Scientists working with such subjects take advantage of the fact that with a large enough sample of humans or animals the differences between them due to genetics or experience cancel out. As an illustration, a large sample of children, if randomly selected, will include ones from all racial, economic, and social groups and will include some, for example, who were reared with strict discipline and some who were reared leniently; thus the effects of background group and type of rearing on their responses will cancel out when the sample is viewed as a whole.

Many of the factors giving rise to a behavior are set by the scientist at the time of the experiment. For example, the experimenter can place a monkey in a testing chamber in which he can press a lever to view either another monkey or a model of a monkey as a measure of his attachment to the two objects. In this case, it is possible to specify quite precisely the physical arrangement and the amount of immediate prior experience with the two objects. A scientist attempts to describe the situation so completely that someone else, when reading of the experiment, could duplicate it exactly.

The last point brings us to a central goal in scientific work—**repeatability**. By repeatability we mean the possibility of another scientist's performing the same experiment to verify or invalidate the original findings. The ability of science to describe and explain the natural world rests upon the dis-

covery of universal natural laws that explain some facet of the
world. If the repetition of an experiment results in the same
findings, then the original observation is given more credence,
and if it is never found wanting, it will become part of our
"fund of knowledge" regarding the natural world.

There are two basic methods of scientific investigation.
One is termed the "field method" and the other is the "laboratory method"—both are valid means of discovering the
nature of the world. The **field method** entails the observation of a phenomenon in its natural setting—that is, in the
field. This method is exemplified in the work of Jane Van
Lawick-Goodall, who spent many years in the African jungles
observing the life and behavior of the chimpanzee. Through
lengthy observation she was able to describe the behavior of
wild chimps and devise generalities regarding their behavior
patterns. The classical field method does not attempt to create
situations for an organism to respond to; rather it permits the
discovery of natural laws by observation of naturally occurring
phenomena. Astronomy is an example of the extensive use of
the field method.

The **laboratory method** rests on the ability of a scientist
to manipulate some facet of the environment and to measure
the result of this manipulation. He controls, as much as possible, all facets of the environment, (which are termed **variables**) except the one whose effect he is interested in. For
example, in a laboratory study of mate preferences among
domestic dogs, he might hypothesize that odor is an important
variable in determining mate preference. The experimenter
would then present male dogs with females differing only in
odor—the other variables, such as size, coloration, and prior
experience, would be the same for all the females. Thus, the
experimenter could say what effect the presence of a particular odor has on mating preference of male dogs. The scientist
has, thus, *controlled* the variables that the dog is confronted
with. **Control** is the distinguishing feature of the laboratory
method. Logically, field study should be able to describe behaviors seen in the natural setting and their probable causes,

whereas the laboratory method should be able precisely to identify the causes and the effect of their manipulation. In practice, however, scientists do not operate in such prescribed areas; rather, they employ both methods in their search for laws of nature. In fact field study is often a prelude to laboratory investigation.

In the study of behavior these two methods can be seen to be emphasized to varying degrees by different groups of scientists. **Ethologists** (those who study animal behavior), who are primarily European and were trained as zoologists, have tended to emphasize the field approach. The laboratory method is emphasized by American scientists who are generally psychologists by training. As with most generalizations this one breaks down with close observation. In any event, the two approaches are complementary one to another.

In this section we have seen that we are all students of behavior. We all analyze, criticize, and complement each others' behavior every day. However, our views of the behavior of people are slanted; they are biased by our prejudices and by our incomplete understanding of situations. Scientific study of behavior attempts to do away with prejudices and biases. One of the critical elements of the scientific investigation of behavior is controlling variables that might affect and influence an experiment. Methods of limiting the genetic and experimental differences among subjects in an experiment were discussed. There are two basic methods of scientific investigation. In the field method organisms are observed in "the wild" where they can perform in their natural habitat, not hampered by the restrictions of a laboratory environment. However, variables can not be controlled very effectively in the field, and thus when a precise examination of one variable is desired, the laboratory method is often chosen. The all-important feature of the laboratory method is the incorporation of controls.

SUGGESTIONS FOR FURTHER READING

Many of the *Scientific American* articles included among these suggestions are available as separate offprints, which may be ordered by number from W. H. Freeman and Company, 660 Market Street, San Francisco, California 94104.

Agranoff, B. W. Memory and Protein Synthesis, *Scientific American*, June 1967. (Offprint 1077)

DiCara, L. V. Learning in the Autonomic Nervous System, *Scientific American*, January 1970. (Offprint 525)

Gerard, R. W. What Is Memory? *Scientific American*, September 1953. (Offprint 11)

Hockett, C. F. The Origin of Speech, *Scientific American*, September 1960. (Offprint 603)

Lorenz, K. Z. The Evolution of Behavior, *Scientific American*, December 1958. (Offprint 412)

Lorenz, K. Z. *King Solomon's Ring*. New York: Crowell, 1952.

Luria, A. R. The Functional Organization of the Brain, *Scientific American*, March 1970. (Offprint 526)

Morris, D. *The Naked Ape*. New York: McGraw-Hill, 1967.

Premack, A. J., and Premack, D. Teaching Language to an Ape, *Scientific American*, October 1972. (Offprint 549)

Pribram, K. H. The Neurophysiology of Remembering, *Scientific American*, January 1969. (Offprint 520)

Skinner, B. F. How to Teach Animals, *Scientific American*, December 1951. (Offprint 423)

Tinbergen, N. The Curious Behavior of the Stickleback, *Scientific American*, December 1952. (Offprint 414)

2

BIOLOGICAL BASES OF BEHAVIOR

BEHAVIOR AS MOVEMENT

All behavior, as commonly defined, is muscle movement or glandular secretion. Try to imagine a behavior expressed via any other means. You cannot. As we will see, scientists often define behavior more broadly, to include, for instance, the activity of brain cells. This broad definition is somewhat misleading, for an observer could not detect the "behavior" without the aid of highly sophisticated surgical techniques and electronics. As our main "behavioral output" proceeds from the muscular system, we shall examine it briefly.

The function of any muscle is to contract. Skeletal muscles are attached to the bony skeleton by tough tendons and move the skeleton by contracting. A muscle can only contract or pull; it cannot push. Therefore, a reversal in the direction of a movement of the arm, for example, must come about by the contraction of a second set of muscles. As a moment's reflection will confirm, most muscles in the human body exist in pairs—termed extensors and flexors. These functional groups of muscles work in a highly coordinated manner, yet are highly antagonistic, that is, they produce opposite results. Proponents of isometric exercises take advantage of the antagonistic nature of muscles and base an exercise program on the simultaneous activation of flexors and extensors—the net result is no movement, but considerable expenditure of energy.

A muscle, such as the familiar biceps, consists of many small cylindrical fibers, each capable of independent contraction. Peering at a muscle fiber under the extremely high magnification of the electron microscope, the observer is struck by the orderly geometric pattern and the presence of tiny tubes within the fiber. These tiny tubes, the **myofibrils** (literally meaning "muscle fibrils"), are only a micron in diameter (one micron is 1/1,000,000 of a meter or 1/25,000 of an inch). The myofibrils are built of two proteins. During muscular contraction the two proteins slide past one another, resulting in a shortening of the myofibril (Fig. 6).

Muscular contraction and thus most behavior is based on untold trillions of protein molecules sliding past one another. Muscles do not operate by themselves; they require input from the nervous system to provoke contraction (although some muscles, such as the smooth muscle of the intestine and the heart muscle, can contract rhythmically in the absence of neural input). The nervous system influences muscle by messages sent along nerves. A **nerve** comprises the long extensions (which are often called processes) of many nerve cells, or **neurons**. The **cell bodies**, enlarged regions of the neurons that contain the nuclei, usually lie within the brain or the spinal cord. The nerve supplying a limb muscle, for example, has its origin in the spinal cord (Fig. 7). In particular, it is only the type of neuron process called an **axon** that makes the

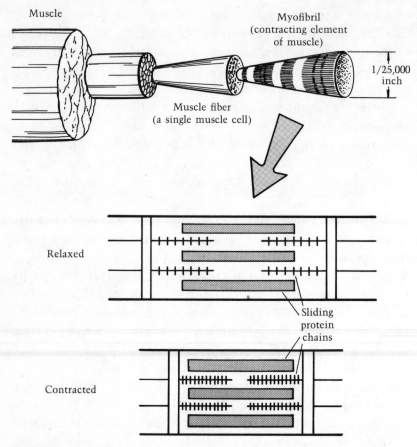

Muscle

Myofibril
(contracting element
of muscle)

1/25,000
inch

Muscle fiber
(a single muscle cell)

Relaxed

Sliding
protein
chains

Contracted

Figure 6 An artist's conception of the contracting elements within a muscle. The myofibril contains two different kinds of protein chains that, when the muscle is activated, slide past one another resulting in the contraction of the muscle.

lengthy journey from the cell body to a muscle, and a nerve is thus a bundle of axons. The neuron causes the muscle to contract by means of a chemical released from the end of the axon. This chemical transmits the message calling for contraction from nerve to muscle. This chemical **transmitter** acts on the muscle to cause the proteins to slide past one another. A spinal cord neuron does not have much of "a mind of its own" and thus must, in turn, rely on other parts of the ner-

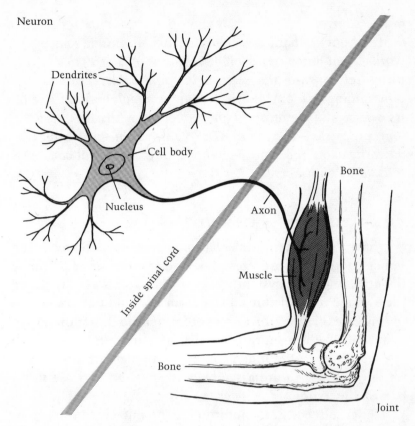

Figure 7 Nerve–muscle relationships. A neuron, originating inside the spinal cord, communicates with the muscle by means of a long axon. The axon thus is the output end of the neuron. Input to the neuron arrives via the dendrites and the cell body.

vous system for most commands to contract the muscle it controls. The spinal cord is, however, rather good at such simple jobs as reflex reactions to painful stimuli. Facial muscles are controlled by similar neurons that are located in the base of the brain rather than in the spinal cord.

In this short section we have seen that the behavior of man or of any animal is expressed by his muscles. We have come to understand a bit of the operation of the muscles and of the controlling influences that direct the muscles. A good deal is known about the structure of the muscle and how it works, even down to the chemical basis of contraction, which ultimately entails the seemingly improbable action of proteins sliding past one another. A nerve supplying a muscle has its origin elsewhere and communicates with the muscle by long processes—the axons. The neuron transmits a message down its axon, releasing a chemical at the end that causes the muscle to contract.

THE NEURON AS GLAND

We have seen that muscles are controlled by chemical substances, termed transmitters, released from neurons. Actually, the entire nervous system works in the same way—by the release of a chemical transmitter from the tip of an axon that, in this case, has an effect on another neuron rather than upon a muscle. The transmitters are manufactured in the cell body and travel down the long axon to accumulate in tiny packets for later release or are assembled at the site of release in the end of the axon.

The cell body, in addition to manufacturing of transmitter, contains many structures necessary to the continued health and well-being of the cell. The most prominent structure, the nucleus, contains the genetic information required to build the cell in the form of deoxyribonucleic acid (DNA). In fact, the DNA within any nucleus carries enough genetic information to specify the building of an entire organism. This fact has led biologists to attempt to recreate an individual organism from a single cell. To date these efforts, known as **cloning**, have been successful with plants and frogs. In cloning the DNA is removed from the cell of a mature organism and placed into an egg cell of another organism. The transplanted DNA contains the genetic information required to "build" an organism identical to the donor. By placing the DNA of ten cells from a single frog into ten host egg cells, ten frogs identical to the donor can be produced. If it becomes possible to clone man, the possibilities for producing multiple copies of humans will have to be dealt with. Scores of Einsteins are a far different matter than scores of Hitlers!

The cytoplasm surrounding the nucleus contains several other specialized structures; among them are ribosomes (sites of protein manufacture), golgi bodies (probable sites of transmitter manufacture), and mitochondria (sites of conversion of food and oxygen into cellular energy). A complex network of minute tubes interlaces the cytoplasm, extending into the fine extensions of the neuron. These tubes are thought to transport materials within the cell. A membrane surrounds the cytoplasm. The structure of the membrane is such that it allows certain material to pass into or out of the cytoplasm. This selective passage of materials is essential to cellular metabolism and excretion in general and for the operation of the nervous system.

Several other fine extensions of the neuron, in addition to the axon, are shown in Figure 7, and these are finely branched. They are **dendrites**. Just as axons carry "messages" away from the cell body, the dendrites convey information to the cell body. Contacts coming from other neurons are made primarily on the dendrites and secondarily on the cell body itself; contacts are rarely made on the axon. Thus, incoming information travels via dendrites, and outgoing information via axons. We have been using the word "contacts" to describe the communication between two neurons. To be accurate, the neurons do not actually touch; rather there is an almost infinitesimally small (1/50,000,000 of a meter) gap between the axon of one and the dendrite (or cell body) of another. This gap is called, the **synapse**. The transmitter is released from storage packets in the end of the axon into the synapse where it has an effect on the opposing dendrite or cell body. A transmitter released by the axon of a neuron can do one of two things: it may arouse (excite) or it may depress (inhibit) the action of the adjoining neuron (Fig. 8).

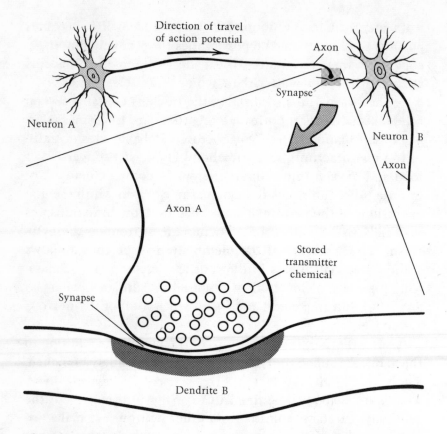

Figure 8 Synapse. Neuron A communicates with neuron B via a synapse between an axon and a dendrite. The expanded part of the illustration shows the synapse, which is actually a tiny gap separating the membranes of the two neurons. Transmitter chemical stored in tiny packets in the axon is released into the synapse upon the arrival of an action potential. The transmitter chemical then either excites or inhibits the activity of neuron B.

Transmitter is released when a nerve impulse arrives at the end of the axon from its point of origin in the cell body. We measure the nerve impulse as a voltage moving down the axon at speeds of up to 100 meters per second (which is far short of the speed of electricity—namely, 300,000,000 meters per second). The voltage, however, is merely a convenient by-product of the nerve impulse: "convenient" in that it can be recorded and measured by scientists. The nerve impulse itself, usually called an **action potential**, is a transient alteration in the cell membrane that allows a brief flow of ions (electrically charged chemical components of cytoplasm) across it. The "potential" in the term is short for potential difference— the electric charge of some point relative to the electric charge of some other point. The action potential travels down the axon to release transmitter at the tip of the axon. The action potential has been compared to a fuse used on explosives. Once lit it will burn at a constant rate down the length of the fuse. Although a burning fuse is like an axon in that the changes in both are chemical reactions, the axon can be "used" again and again, whereas a fuse can be burned only once.

A neuron will "fire" (conduct an action potential down its axon) when the cell body has been sufficiently aroused or excited by the input it receives. As a cell receives both excitatory and inhibitory input, often simultaneously, it will fire only when the total amount of excitatory transmitter input exceeds by a critical amount the total amount of inhibitory transmitter input. Once the critical amount is reached, there is an action potential (Fig. 9).

Thus, each of our 10 billion neurons has two kinds of input that together determine whether it will fire, and each of these neurons communicates with about 1,000 other cells. All of this is the more amazing when we realize that all behaviors, thoughts, and feelings are the result of the basically simple relations between individual neurons multiplied millions, or even billions, of times. Indeed, the tremendous mass of minutiae that we remember and carry with us is also laid down and read out, if not stored, in this elementary manner. It is somewhat surprising, considering their awesome task, that we are not capable of replacing damaged neurons. Once lost, they are not regenerated. You never have more brain cells than at the day of your birth. In fact, they are dying off at the rate of thousands per day—never to be replaced. This is one of the factors producing senility in old age.

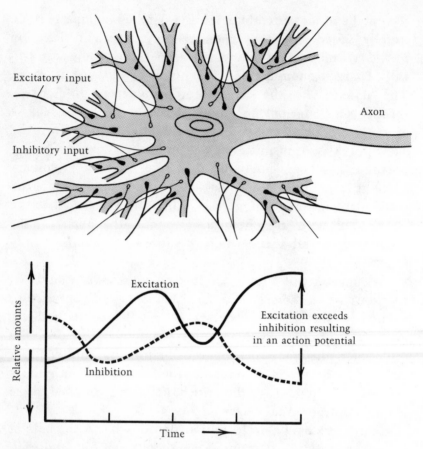

Figure 9 Neural input. Most neurons receive input—both inhibitory and excitatory—from both excitatory and inhibitory sources. Whether an action potential is produced in a neuron at any particular moment depends upon the relative excitation and inhibition. Only when excitation exceeds inhibition is an action potential generated.

It is hoped that the title of this section "Neuron as Gland" is now clear. For, in a very real sense, it is perfectly acceptable to view each individual neuron as a secreting gland whose product (the transmitter) plays a specific role (initiation of an action potential) analogous to the salivary *gland, whose specific role in the first stages of digestion is to secrete salivary fluid into the mouth.*

A neuron is like any other cell in the body in that it needs to receive oxygen and food, and eliminate waste products. In addition, it is specialized for the transmission of information. It does this by means of unique structures within the cell, dendrites and axons, and by specialized contacts between cells, the synapses. We have seen how neurons can have either excitatory or inhibitory effect on adjacent cells, and how the net result of excitation or inhibition may be the production of an action potential that, upon arrival at the end of an axon, releases a chemical transmitter that either excites or inhibits the next cell in line. In a real sense then the neuron is a tiny secreting gland.

COLLECTIONS OF NEURONS

The brain of any sophisticated organism (and quite a few rather unsophisticated ones) is considerably more than a loose collection of neurons. The brain is rigidly organized and specialized. By way of analogy, a large corporation is composed of many departments, such as personnel, purchasing, shipping, and executive. Each department has a specific job to do, and a chart may be drawn of the organization showing lines of command and communication. So it is with the brain. There are departments concerned with decoding information about the world. Other departments process the information and arrive at "executive decisions" regarding a course of action, and still other departments function to set the muscles of the organism into operation. One of the goals of the neurosciences is to identify the "departments" within the brain and their "lines of command."

Perhaps the best way to understand the incredibly complex puzzle presented by the numerous specialized regions of the brain and the interconnections between them is to understand something of the development of the brain. We can

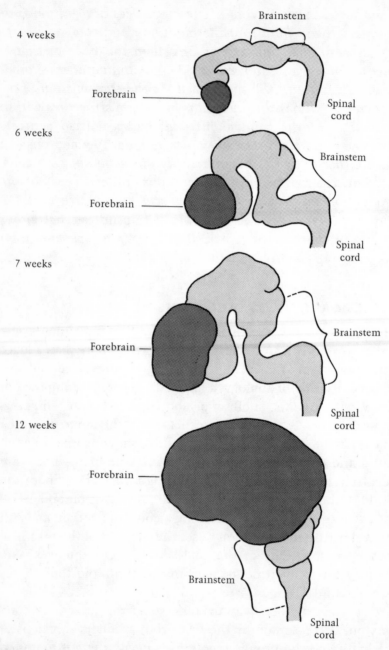

Figure 10 The development of the human brain. These drawings (not to scale) made from human embryos of ages noted, show the development of three of the basic neural structures in the brain.

view this development from two perspectives: by observing changes in an individual brain from conception to maturity or by comparing the brain of man with those of progressively simpler organisms. Drawings of the developing human brain in a few embryological stages (Fig. 10) show some basic structures: the spinal cord, the brainstem, and forebrain. These basic structures of the brain are elaborated, enlarged, and in some animals, engulfed during development. The brainstem, for example, is very much overshadowed by the various forebrain structures in the developing human brain. In fact, as will be seen below, the tremendous development of the forebrain is a feature crucial in making man what he is—the most ascendant of species!

Now consider the brains of simpler organisms in relation to the brain of man (Fig. 11). As we proceed from simple (fish) to complex (cat) we note that the forebrain becomes tremendously enlarged relative to the other areas of the brain.

The brain is not an amorphous mass of tissue. Rather, it is subdivided into an array of components. We shall briefly identify and outline the functions of the major of these brain divisions. Basically your nervous system, like that of the earthworm, fish, and cat, consists of a concentrated mass of neural tissue (the **central nervous system**, which includes the brain) and a widely distributed system of nerves and receptors (the **peripheral nervous system**).

Peripheral Nervous System

The peripheral nervous system consists of the nerves connecting skin, muscles, and various organs to the brain. These nerves carry sensory information about the body and about the external world to the brain. The nerves of the peripheral nervous system also carry motor commands to the muscles, glands, and organs of the body. Actually, the peripheral nervous system performs two quite different jobs, and it is thus subdivided into two systems. One type of function is related to keeping all the machinery of the body working properly and making adjustments for changing demands upon the

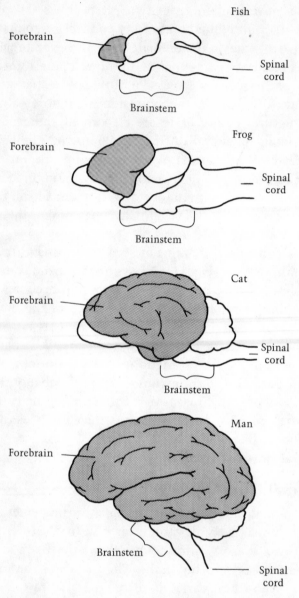

Figure 11 Brains of fish, frog, cat, and man. Brainstem and spinal cord structures are relatively similar in all four species. As evolution proceeded from fish to man, the forebrain became tremendously enlarged, eventually engulfing the brainstem. (The drawings are not to scale.)

body. The nerves having this type of function, which supply the heart, kidney, liver, gastrointestinal tract, and circulatory system of the body, operate very much on their own—we generally do not pay much attention to our heart rate or blood pressure (unless we are hypochondriacs), yet the system is continually changing to accommodate the demands the central nervous system puts upon it.

For instance, when we run up a flight of stairs our heart rate increases and the blood flow to our muscles increases to supply them with oxygen, yet we are generally unaware of these changes—until, that is, we arrive at the top of the stairs with our heart pounding. This subdivision of the peripheral nervous system is termed the **autonomic nervous system** (Fig. 12). Students occasionally misread autonomic and come up with "automatic nervous system," which would not be a bad name as the system operates with little conscious help from us. It should be emphasized that simply because we, as members of Western society, cannot modify at will the actions of the autonomic nervous system, it doesn't follow that it is impossible to do so. Many Eastern societies, which emphasize introspection more than do Western ones, can provide examples of persons capable of altering their autonomic functions at will. You have, no doubt, heard of individuals who claim to be able to stop their hearts, walk on hot embers, or stick pins through their skin without pain or bleeding. These persons have learned how to modify autonomic functions.

The autonomic nervous system works very much as do the accelerator and the brake on an automobile. Part of it works to increase heart rate, blood flow, or other vital functions, and part to decrease heart rate and blood flow. In the autonomic nervous system, however, often both the "accelerator" and the "brake" are being applied at the same time. Now, if we were to drive an automobile in this manner (and some people do!), speed (or whether there were any motion at all) would depend on the relative force applied to the accelerator and the brake. In the autonomic nervous system the

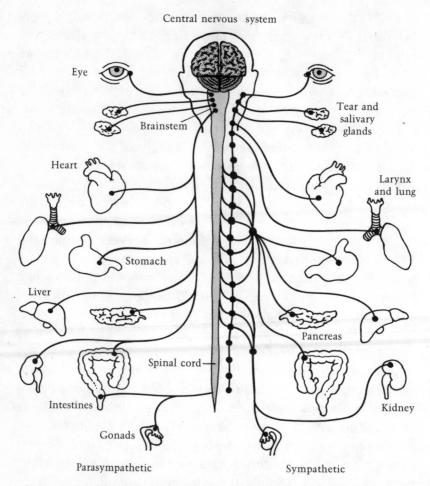

Central nervous system

Eye

Brainstem

Tear and salivary glands

Heart

Larynx and lung

Stomach

Liver

Pancreas

Spinal cord

Intestines

Kidney

Gonads

Parasympathetic

Sympathetic

Figure 12 Sympathetic and parasympathetic divisions of the autonomic nervous system and the organs that they innervate. Only half of each division of the autonomic nervous system is shown. Both divisions supply organs on both sides of the body.

"accelerator" is termed the **sympathetic division** and the "brake" is the **parasympathetic division**. Generally, one or the other is predominant, the sympathetic, which functions to mobilize overall bodily resources for action, or the parasympathetic, which functions to conserve and maintain specific bodily resources.

The other subdivision of the peripheral nervous system, which is called the **somatic nervous system**, is responsible for what we usually call "behavior." That is, messages for voluntary movements are conveyed by this part of the peripheral nervous system from the brain to muscle and sensations are conveyed by it from receptors to the brain. The somatic nervous system, like the autonomic, consists of both sensory and motor nerves, and *unlike* the autonomic nervous system, is more-or-less under our conscious control.

Central Nervous System

The central nervous system can be conveniently divided into three parts: spinal cord, brainstem, and forebrain. The brainstem and forebrain can each be further subdivided into several functional groups. In the sections below each of the major parts and their subdivisions will be discussed.

Spinal cord. The **spinal cord** of man is about the diameter of your little finger and is primarily responsible for the routing of commands between the brain and the body. The other major task of the spinal cord is protecting the body from tissue damage by reflexes of various sorts. Examples include the knee-jerk reflex and the withdrawal reflex elicited by placing your hand on a hot stove. Reflexive behavior is controlled by the spinal cord without the direct participation of the brain (actually, the distinction between spinal cord and brain is a hazy one at best—the two appear similar under the microscope). Considering the rather crucial nature of its job, it is no surprise that the spinal cord is afforded a considerable amount of protection. A fluid-filled sack encases the spinal cord, as well as the brain, and acts as a "shock absorber." A similar principle is at work in protecting a developing human in the womb of its mother.

The spinal cord is encased in a bony skeleton, the **vertebrae**, which offers considerable mechanical support and protection. Nevertheless, occasionally the protective devices are overstrained, resulting in a break in the spinal cord.

When this occurs, the region of the body below the break is both analgesic (without feeling) and paralyzed. If the spinal cord was not extensively damaged in the break then the paralyzed area will and does respond on a reflexive level, although the victim may not be aware of the actions of his limbs because of the analgesia.

The spinal cord is a relatively simple part of the central nervous system, yet it contains all of the cell types found in the brain itself, and because of this, has proved to be a valuable tool or "model" of the infinitely more complex brain. Cell types within the brain and the spinal cord are (1) **sensory neurons**—cells concerned with bringing information into the central nervous system; (2) **interneurons**—cells whose job is to process information between input and output; and (3) **motor neurons**—cells that receive information from either sensory neurons or interneurons and in turn activate the output apparatus—muscle or gland (Fig. 13). The brain of man is composed, basically, of these three cell types, with interneurons far outnumbering the other two. A brain interneuron is not much different from a spinal cord interneuron, nor, for that matter is a human interneuron much different from a salamander interneuron. It is quite true that we can view the phenomena of man not as the consequence of having a brain, which all advanced organisms have, nor of simply possessing interneurons, but of having a brain that consists of many more interneurons with much more intricate interconnections than any other species.

Brainstem. For our purposes the **brainstem** refers to a collection of structures located at the base of the brain. These structures are present in, and very similar across, a wide range of organisms. As relatively primitive organisms have these structures their functions are probably relatively primitive or basic. A posterior portion of the brainstem contains areas whose function is to regulate heart rate, blood pressure, respiration, and stomach and intestinal contraction. These areas

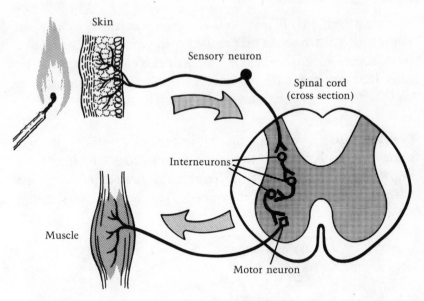

Skin

Sensory neuron

Spinal cord
(cross section)

Interneurons

Muscle

Motor neuron

Figure 13 Sensations on the surface of the skin conducted into the spinal cord by a sensory neuron. Numerous interneurons relay the information to a motor neuron that when activated causes a muscle to contract. This simply reflex arc protects us from damaging stimuli. Note that the participation of the brain is not required.

are associated with the autonomic nervous system. Also found in the posterior-brainstem bundles are various sensory and motor axons that extend down into the spinal cord.

Reticular formation. Ascending up through the brainstem is a structure whose discovery made a major impact on the brain sciences in the 1940's. The **reticular formation** is a diffuse collection of neurons ascending from the spinal cord into the cortex. It has a portion that influences motor responses and a portion involved with incoming sensory information. In fact, all incoming sensory information is routed via the reticular formation before reaching the specific sensory decoding areas on the cortex. It has been suggested that the reticular formation, from which axons go out to all parts of the cortex, functions to alert or focus the attention of an organism (Fig. 14). It may well be activity in the reticular formation of your pet cat that causes it to come running from a considerable distance at the sound of the can opener, a stimulus that has great significance to the cat. Most anesthetics and tranquilizers act upon this brainstem structure.

Cerebellum.   Overlying the brainstem is another phylogenetically ancient structure—the **cerebellum**. It has been known for centuries that the cerebellum has something to do with the coordination of movement, yet the means by which

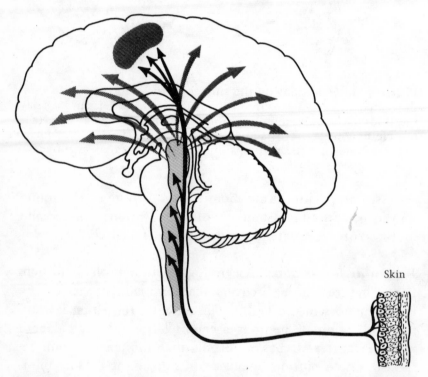

Skin

Figure 14 The reticular activating system. Sensory information coming up into the brain influences the reticular activating system so that the entire forebrain is aroused. In addition, specific sensory information is routed to the appropriate cortical sensory area. Adapted from "The Reticular Formation" by J. D. French. Copyright © 1957 by Scientific American, Inc. All rights reserved.)

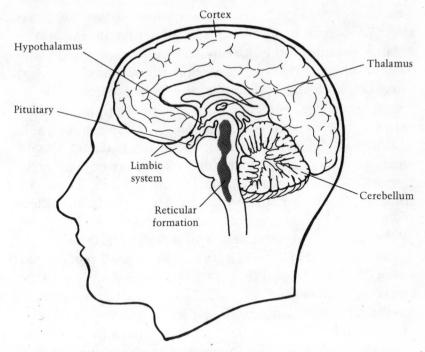

Figure 15 A cross section of the brain of man. Shown are several of the structures referred to in the text.

it operated was unknown. Recently, scientists have gained considerable insight into the "wiring diagram" of the cerebellum. As is true in most scientific endeavors in which something is investigated more and more closely, the picture may become more and more complex. Yet it is the hope that the recent discoveries regarding the organization and function of the cerebellum and adjacent structures foreshadow significant breakthroughs in our understanding of brain function.

Forebrain.   The greatest bulk of the brain of man is the *forebrain*. This portion of the central nervous system finds its greatest elaboration in man. The forebrain consists of the thalamus, hypothalamus and pituitary, limbic system, and cortex. Each of these areas will be discussed below.

Thalamus. The incoming sensory information that was seen to pass by way of the reticular formation finds its way to a large structure—the **thalamus**. This consists of a large number of nuclei whose job entails the relaying of sensory information to the appropriate area of the cortex. The incoming sensory information is then further processed in the cortex, as we shall see later. The thalamus also receives information sent down from the cortex. In the thalamus specific areas are associated with the different forms of sensory information—vision, hearing, touch, and so forth. This brain structure is indispensable to the human species, for without it we would be incapable of vision, hearing, or feeling.

A quite different function is served by a collection of thalamic areas that receive information from all types of sensation. These nonspecific areas have axons going up to the cortex as well as to other places. Unlike the sensory-specific relay nuclei, they have axons spreading through the entirety of the cortex rather than limiting their output to the specific cortical sensory area. The function of this nonspecific part of the thalamus appears to parallel the functions of the reticular formation. Thus, it is involved in awakening or arousing the rest of the brain, and hence the organism, into a state of focused attention on a relevant event in the environment. This area also plays an important role in the processes of sleep and wakefulness.

Hypothalamus. If a person were ever to undertake a search for the functional "center of the brain" the logical candidate would have to be the **hypothalamus**. It is a tiny structure buried in the base of the brain. It, like the thalamus, is composed of many nuclei, and each nucleus of the hypothalamus has a specific duty. There are nuclei associated with eating, drinking, sexual behavior, body temperature and fluid balance, sleeping, waking, and in general, emotional behavior of various sorts. An organism deprived of its hypothalamus is incapable of regulating these activities and soon dies.

Pituitary.   The hypothalamus, in addition to having the duties listed above, is also quite intimately associated with the master gland of the body—the **pituitary**. The pituitary lies immediately below the hypothalamus, and a thin stalk of neural tissue connects the two. Thus, brain (hypothalamus) meets gland (pituitary). The marriage is a happy one with the functions of brain and gland complementing one another in what is really a single functional system. Our distinctions between muscle and bone, skin and brain, plant and animal, nerve and gland are often creations of our own imagination and perspective. The categories into which we sort parts of an organism often do not hold up when examined closely. An example of this is provided by the hypothalamus, a structure considered to be a part of the brain, but which manufactures chemicals that are then transported to the pituitary for release into the blood stream.

Limbic system.   The last major region of the brain beneath the cortex is the **limbic system**. As the name implies, it is a collection of many individual structures (including the hippocampus, amygdala, septum) that are thought to operate as a single functional system. The limbic system is currently being subjected to concerted study by brain scientists in an attempt to reveal its function. So far our understanding of the limbic system is very incomplete. However, all scientists agree that the limbic system appears to be involved in emotionality, motivation, and perhaps, aggression and memory.

Cortex.   The **cortex** of man is a wrinkled layer of brain tissue lying immediately beneath the skull and surrounding most of the structures mentioned previously. Of all the cells in the brain of man, about three-fourths are found in the cortex. It is easy to assume from this that the cortex is performing many tasks that require much neural "machinery." The picture of a large enveloping cortex does not hold for all organisms, however. The amphibians and fish have no cortex, and birds and reptiles have only a minute amount. From species to species, going up the phylogenetic scale, the amount of cortex increases dramatically. Thus, it is apparent that the cortex is not necessary to life. In fact, humans suffering from a misfortune of nature are occasionally born lacking a cortex, and they may live; their behavior, however, is limited to very primitive responses.

"Man," used in its broadest connotation, is the end product of the activity of his cortex. What, then, are the functions served by the cortex?

The cortical surface is composed of a thin layer of neurons (about the thickness of a phonograph record). In less sophisticated organisms, such as the rat, the cortex is a smooth covering enveloping the rest of the brain. In man and the higher organisms the smooth cortical surface has become in-

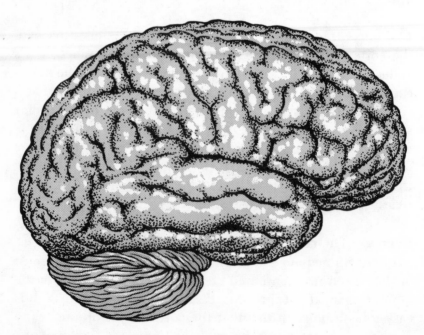

Figure 16 A drawing of the surface of the human brain. The cortex is greatly infolded with more than half of the surface hidden from view.

folded and thus much increased in surface area. It is estimated that at least 60 percent of the surface of man's cortex is hidden from view in the infolded areas (termed the sulci, as opposed to the "hills," or gyri) (Fig. 16).

Within the cortex there are numerous subdivisions. The most obvious is that which forms the *hemispheres*, left and right. Many subcortical structures are thus present in the brain as pairs, one in the right hemisphere and one in the left. Each hemisphere is further divided into four lobes, which more or less correspond to major landmarks on the surface of the brain. They are the **frontal**, **parietal**, **temporal**, and **occipital lobes** (Fig. 17).

Each of these four lobes contains yet further subdivisions. The parietal, temporal, and occipital lobes receive sensory

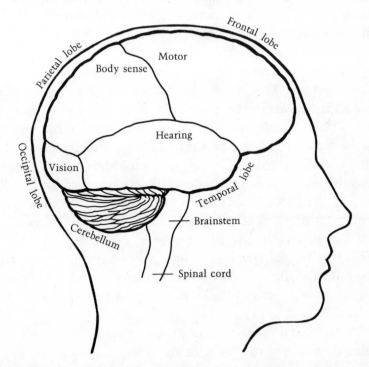

Figure 17 The four lobes of the right hemisphere of the cortex. The left hemisphere is similarly divided into four lobes.

information from "body senses," hearing, and vision, respectively. These sensory-receiving areas occupy a small portion of each lobe, the remainder being termed the **"association" cortex**, because presumably this is the region where the basic associating of one thing with another is done. Each sensory area of the cortex is laid out in a **receptortopic** pattern. That is, the visual-receiving area in the occipital lobe processes sensations received by the retina, the auditory-receiving area in the temporal lobe processes sensations received by the cochlea, and the body-sense–receiving area in the parietal lobe processes sensations received by the body surface.

To appreciate this organization, consider for a moment the body senses. Touch, pressure, temperature, muscle sense and position sense are included in the body senses. Thus, input from all parts of the body surface (and interior) are represented in this sensory modality. The map onto the brain of this information is symbolically represented in Figure 18. An obvious question comes to mind as we look at this illustration: why is the figure so distorted, why are the hands and mouth so exaggerated? The answer is that cortical area in the brain is allocated in accordance with the fineness of sensation possible. Thus, the parts of our bodies that are the most sensitive are the hands and lips, and they, correspondingly, have a large cortical area for the processing of their sensations. There is a point-to-point representation from a receptor (retina, cochlea, skin) to the specific sensory-receiving area of the cortex, and an amount of cortical area proportional to the fineness of discrimination possible by that receptor. We will come back to this point in our discussion of sensory systems. Note from Figure 19 that the sensory and motor pathways of the brain are crossed, that is, sensations from the *right* hand are registered in the *left* hemisphere.

The frontal lobe plays a crucial role in the sending of motor impulses to the muscles via the spinal cord. The motor area, which occupies part of the frontal lobe, is built analogously to the sensory areas. In this case the cortical surface

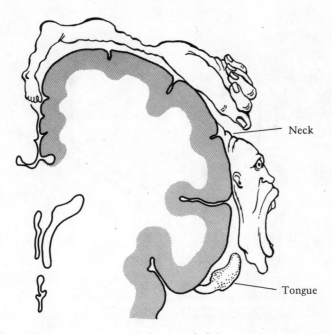

Neck

Tongue

Figure 18 Representation of area of the somatic sensory cortex for the function of various body parts. This is a representation of the left side of the body on the right hemisphere of the brain. The area for a body part is proportional to the sensitivity of that part; thus the enlarged hands and lips.

represents muscles rather than receptors. The strategy is the same—a greater area for parts of the musculature that are capable of fine, precise movement. Thus, the hands and mouth regions here too are disproportionately large. In fact, the body-sense–receiving area (in the parietal lobe) and the motor area (in the frontal lobe), which are physically adjacent, are mirror images of one another.

The sensory and motor areas of man's cortex are rather small compared with the association areas, which are neither sensory nor motor. The association areas no doubt serve the complex behavioral responses of which higher organisms are capable. They are involved in complex learning and memory tasks, and as we shall see later, are necessary for the production and understanding of language. The association areas

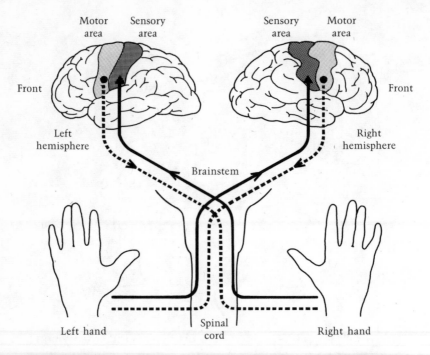

Figure 19 Crossed motor and sensory pathways of the brain. Sensations from the right hand are registered in the left hemisphere; sensations from the left hand are registered in the right hemisphere. This is generally true for all sensations. Motor commands to the right hand or leg are similarly generated in the motor area of the left hemisphere. (Adapted from "The Asymmetry of the Human Brain" by D. Kimura. Copyright © 1973 by Scientific American, Inc. All rights reserved.)

increase tremendously in importance as species increasingly higher in the phylogenetic scale are considered. Figure 20 depicts the absolute size differences between the brains of several species and the relative amount of cortical association areas. It is obvious that the association areas of man's brain outshadow those of any other species.

Although brain scientists are still trying to delineate the precise functions of the association areas, several discoveries have furthered our knowledge of these areas. One of the most exciting discoveries concerns the functions of the speech areas

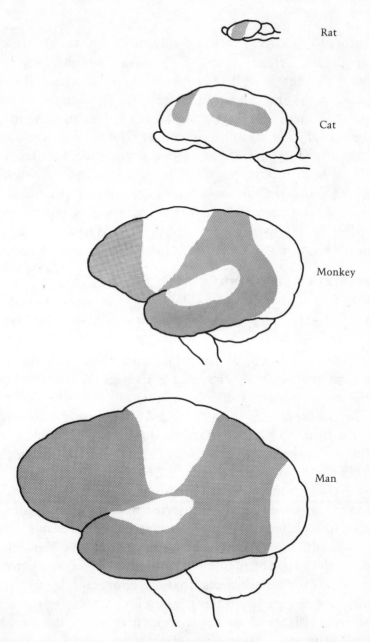

Figure 20 Rough scale drawings of the cortical hemispheres of four mammals. Note both greater size and the relatively larger association cortex (stippled area) in higher species.

in the dominant hemisphere. (Generally, one hemisphere is dominant—usually the left hemisphere on a right-handed individual.) Portions of the temporal and frontal association areas have been described as speech areas—locations that are crucial in the interpretation of language (spoken or written), as well as in the production of language (verbal or written). Humans who, suffering from various kinds of accidents, have lost portions of the speech areas, experience a number of difficulties in interpreting or generating speech (see also page 120). In short, the cortex is responsible for all higher mental functions and such by-products of the complex interrelations of these functions as society and culture. Without his cortex, man's behavior is reduced to a primitive bundle of reflexes.

The Brain as a Walnut

To understand the design of the brain, you might find it useful to consider an analogy: Picture, if you will, a walnut—in its shell. The meat of the walnut is protected inside a tough shell, much the same as our delicate brain is surrounded by a bony, protective skull. The meat of the walnut is covered by a thin, tightly adhering membrane just as the brain is covered by several such membranes, called **meninges**. These membranes, three in number, have fluid between them and act as "shock absorbers" for the brain. In addition the membranes supply the brain with blood.

A cursory inspection of the nutmeat shows it to consist of two very wrinkled halves connected by a stalk. If the surface area of the nutmeat were to be compared with that of a ball of the same diameter, that of the nutmeat would be many times greater than that of the ball. The brain also is constructed of two halves, or hemispheres, that are connected by a stalk of neural tissue (the brainstem). The outer surface of the brain (the cortex) is wrinkled or convoluted, just as is the walnut's.

Making an analogy between a walnut and the human brain is hardly a new idea. In the seventeenth century the English herbalist William Coles wrote, "Walnuts have the perfect signature of the head: the outer husk or green covering represents the Pericranium or outward skin of the skull, whereon the hair groweth, and therefore salts made of those husks or barks are exceedingly good for wounds in the head. The inner woody shell hath the signature of the skull and the little yellow skin or fell that covers the kernel of the hard Meninga and Pia-Mater, which are the thin surfaces which envelop the brain. The kernel hath the very figure of the brain, and therefore it is very preferable for the brain and resists poisons; for if the kernel be bruised and moistened with the quintescence of wine, and laid upon the crown of the head, it comforts the brain and head mightily." From the middle ages through Cole's day, the resemblance had been taken to be God's indication for man's benefit that the walnut was medicine for ills of the brain. If today we are no longer able to believe in such curative powers, we can, nevertheless, put the walnut to use as a physical model of the brain.

The brain is composed of billions of individual neurons that are gathered together in functional groups. In this section we examined some of these functional groups in terms of three general parts of the brain: (1) the spinal cord, (2) the brainstem, and (3) the forebrain. We looked at the nervous system comparatively from species to species and also in various stages of development and considered functions of various parts of the brain. The autonomic nervous system, comprising the sympathetic division and the parasympathetic division, is a prime controller of our basic life functions. Without it the autonomic bodily machinery of which we are generally unaware, would cease to operate.

The somatic nervous system and the central nervous system are responsible for the expression of our daily behavior, and unlike the autonomic nervous system, are under our voluntary control. We saw that nerve cells are of three kinds: (1) sensory cells, (2) motor cells, and (3) interneurons. Motor and sensory pathways cross from one side of the body to the other side of the brain. The level of sophistication of information processing increases in the structures higher up into the brain, culminating in the cortex, which is highly developed in the human brain in which it is much larger than in that of most other species. The cortical surface is organized into a receptortopic pattern. Each of the four cortical lobes has special jobs.

INPUT TO BRAIN

Much of what we are and do is the result of our interactions with the environment. A major influence on our reaction to the world is the way in which we perceive it. We only know the world via our nervous system. If our nerves convey misinformation, we perceive a distorted picture of the world as reality. Thus, the way in which our nervous system responds to the environment, the way in which it codes sensory information, and the kind of "central processing" the brain does *is* our conception of the world—we have no other.

Vision

Of the sensory systems to be considered here—vision, hearing, touch, and the so-called chemical senses—we know the most about the visual system. The stimuli to which the human eye responds are within a limited segment of the electromagnetic spectrum—namely, the radiation of wavelengths from about 380 to 760 millimicrons. (The total range of wavelengths in the electromagnetic spectrum is from 0.00005 millimicrons to several miles!) This narrow segment of the spectrum contains all the colors seen by the human eye (some animals can see in the infrared and ultraviolet). The eye is not equally sensitive to all colors, being most sensitive to yellow-green as shown in Figure 21.

The human eye is an exquisite, complex sphere, actually a miniature brain in itself. Light enters the eye through the

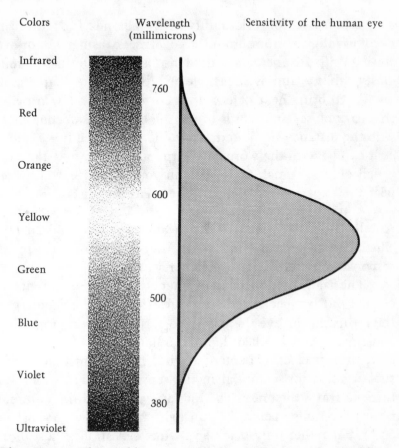

Colors	Wavelength (millimicrons)	Sensitivity of the human eye
Infrared		
	760	
Red		
Orange		
	600	
Yellow		
Green		
	500	
Blue		
Violet		
	380	
Ultraviolet		

Figure 21 The visible portion of the electromagnetic spectrum. The graph shows the relative sensitivity of the human eye to color. (We are most sensitive to yellow-green.)

cornea, a transparent tissue that performs most of the bending of light necessary to form an image on the **retina** (the light-sensitive portion of the eye). The lens, a remarkably elastic, transparent structure, whose construction is similar to an onion, does the final focusing. The image formed on the retina is "upside down and backwards" as a result of passing through the lens. The lens permits precise focusing by changing its shape from spheroid (for close viewing, such as when reading this book) to more flattened (when at rest or focusing on a distant scene). Tiny muscles attached to the edge of the lens are responsible for this ability. Like all muscles, they can become fatigued from prolonged overuse, causing pain or eye strain. With advancing age the lens loses some of its inherent elastic ability and is incapable of changing its shape sufficiently to bring near objects into correct focus. Try bringing this page closer and closer to your eyes. Have someone measure the distance from your eye to the page when it is as close as it can be with the words in sharp focus. Then find a person much older or much younger than you are and have him repeat the experiment. Compare the measured distances.

A transducer changes one form of energy into another. An electric toaster changes electrical energy into heat energy. The nervous system employs a variety of transducers in its response to external forms of energy.

The transduction of light energy into neural activity is carried out by specialized structures (known as receptors) in the retina. In the eye there are two varieties of receptors: **rods** and **cones**. As a result of light stimulation, the receptors generate minute electrical potentials that, if sufficiently large, give rise to an action potential in the sensory neuron, which, in turn, activates the brain. The rods and cones perform different functions. Rods operate in dim light and convey no sense of color, but rather only black and white sensations. Most of us rarely use pure rod vision as in our cities even the nights are too "bright"—a sufficiently dark location would be in the wilderness under a full moon. The receptors you are using at this moment, unless you have rather unusual study habits, are cones. These receptors are responsible for color vision and detailed vision and are operative under all but the dimmest illumination.

Rods and cones are unequally represented over the retina (Fig. 22). A small area directly on the visual axis (the **fovea**, which is the point of fixation when staring at a dot) contains only tightly packed cones. The number of cones falls off rapidly moving along the retina away from the fovea. Rods are thus excluded from the fovea, but appear in large numbers im-

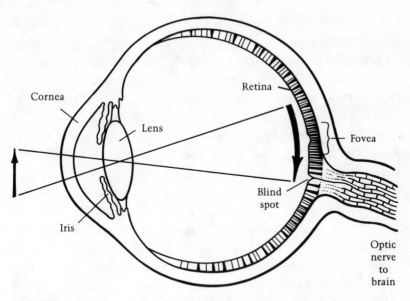

Figure 22 The eye. The focal point on the retina, the fovea, is the region of best detailed vision. The fovea has no rods but has the greatest density of cones. The rods are most dense about 20 degrees away from the fovea. Relative density of rods and cones is indicated. Note that the lens of the eye inverts the image on the retina.

mediately adjacent to it. This concentration of rods just off the visual axis explains the observation by wilderness travelers that a very dim star "cannot be seen" by looking directly at it—the observer must look slightly to the side. The faint light from the star does not activate the cones, but the more sensitive rods.

Both rods and cones contain chemicals that have the unusual property of changing their molecular arrangement upon exposure to light; these are termed **photochemicals**. If you had a test tube full of the rod photochemical and watched it as it was brought out of darkness into light, you would see a change from deep purple to a lighter shade, as if it were being "bleached." This in fact is what is happening, with light doing the "molecular bleaching." If we allowed light to bleach as much of the photochemical as possible (until it stopped becoming paler) and then placed it back into the dark, time would be needed for it to "unbleach" or to reform the original photochemical. Thirty minutes of darkness would reconstitute the test-tube photochemical. This is the same length of time required for a human to establish maximal sensitivity to dim light. There are three varieties of cones, each with its own photochemical: one each for red, green, and blue. Whereas light of almost any wavelength bleaches the rod photochemical, only green light bleaches the cone "green" photochemical. Our awareness of the visual world is determined solely by the actions of the photochemicals as they influence the nervous system.

It is a general rule for all sensory (and motor) systems that most of the information from the right side of the body travels to the left hemisphere of the brain, and vice versa. This generality holds true for the visual system. Visual information from the left half of the field of vision is processed in the right hemisphere, and that from the right visual field is processed in the left hemisphere (see Fig. 23).

When we look at something, its image is projected onto the retina upside down and backwards; the image nonetheless is an accurate representation of the visual world. The projected image activates the rods and cones, and, in turn, the retinal neurons that extend into the brain. This spatial representation of the visual world on the retina is preserved in the cortex in the receptortopic pattern from the retina on the occipital cortex. The fovea has a very large cortical area—no doubt the reason we are capable of seeing much detail from objects in the line-of-sight.

Color vision. Since various combinations of light of the three primary colors (red, green, and blue) will produce any color in the visible spectrum, it is not too surprising that three kinds of cones have been discovered, each being most sensitive to a particular wavelength (and thus to either red, blue, or

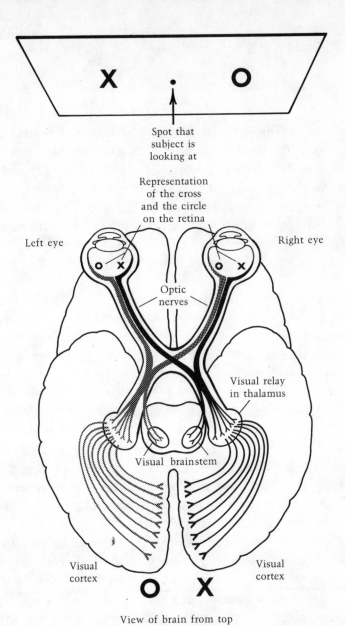

View of brain from top

Figure 23 The visual pathway of man. Images from the right half of the visual field are focused on the left side of each retina. The information from these two left sides travels to the left hemisphere of the brain via a relay in the thalamus. Similarly, images from the left half of the visual field are processed in the right cerebral cortex. The retina also sends axons into the visual area of the brainstem. (Adapted from "The Neurophysiology of Binocular Vision" by J. D. Pettigrew.)

green light). The discovery of the three kinds of cones supports a theory proposed well over one hundred years ago by Young and Helmholtz known as the trichromatic theory of color vision. The brain, however, codes color in terms of the opponent theory of Hering: that is, a neuron responds to two colors by increasing its background firing rate to one and decreasing it to the other. An example of this is a neuron's firing rapidly to red light, inhibiting its firing to green light, and remaining unaffected by yellow or blue light.

Adaptation.   We are all aware that the familiar, the commonplace, doesn't receive much attention—our interest is attracted to the new, the changing, the fashionable. The retina, too, seems to be afflicted with the "Madison Avenue syndrome" in that a constantly moving projection of the world shifts across it because of small, imperceptible movements of the eye. Your eyes are making such movements right now, but you are unaware of it. If these movements were to stop, as in the experiment illustrated in Figure 24, you would not be able to read these words, or in fact see much of anything. This points up a rather important characteristic of most receptors—rapid **adaptation**. By this is meant the tendency to cease responding to a nonchanging stimulus.

That receptors have this property is fortunate for those of us who must wash sweaty gym socks, change diapers, eat someone's terrible cooking, wear clothes, or sit down. The irritation of clothes on your skin or the pressure of the chair upon your buttocks might be unbearable save for rapid receptor adaptation. Indeed it is not likely that you are at this moment aware of the pressure of the clothes on your back; if, however, you think of it or move, thus providing the appropriate stimulus to the receptor—a changing sensory pattern—you may become aware of it.

Visual cortex.   We know something of the way in which the visual system works from experiments in which recordings

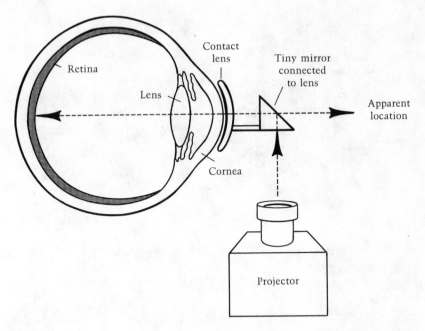

Figure 24 Stabilized image experiment. The small rapid move-ments of the eye are compensated for by a mirror mounted on a contact lens. This prevents the image from moving relative to the retina. The result is greatly impaired vision—the image waxes and wanes and often simply disappears.

were made of the electrical activity of neurons in the visual cortex of cats, whose visual system is much like our own. These experiments by David Hubel and Torsen Weisel showed that single neurons in the cortex respond to very specific kinds of stimuli: moving bars, cubes, or wedges of light projected on a screen (Fig. 25). The visual cortex is organized into regions— in some areas the neurons respond to single stimuli (lines) and in others to more complex stimuli (moving shapes). The same kinds of responses were seen in newborn kittens who had no visual experience prior to the experiment. This rules out the possibility that the neurons developed these response patterns to specific stimuli as a result of experience. The environment, however, can change such inborn response patterns. Young

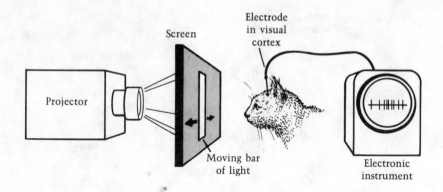

Cell response to moving bar

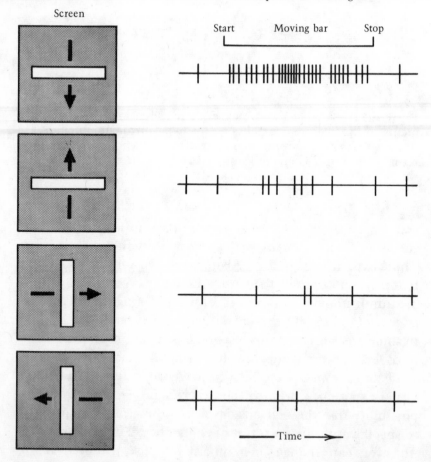

cats were reared in a room containing only horizontal bars. Visual cortex neurons were later examined for responses to horizontal and vertical bars. There were few "vertical neurons" and many "horizontal neurons," implying that the nervous system was functionally changed by an unusual environment.

The importance of these discoveries is that we see the world as we do because our visual system is wired in a certain way. This wiring of the brain seems complete at birth as shown in the kitten study. It now appears likely that our visual perception of the world is in large part genetically determined. Nevertheless, the environment can act upon, and modify, the brain. It thus appears that the visual portion of the brain is genetically prewired but subject to modification by the environment.

Hearing

Hearing, although not as important to man as vision, conveys to our brain a great deal of information about the external world. Like vision, hearing is a sensory system receiving information from distant sources. This is contrasted to touch or taste, wherein direct stimulation of the body surface or interior is conveyed to the brain.

The stimuli that we hear are actually compressions and rarefactions of air molecules, commonly termed sound waves. Figure 26 depicts sound waves created by the forward motion (compression) and backward motion (rarefaction) of the cone of a loudspeaker. Sound waves travel at about 1,000 feet per

---

Figure 25 Visual form reception by single neurons in the visual area of the cortex. A small electrode inserted in the visual cortex of an anesthetized cat picks up discharges of single neurons activated by stimuli presented to the eye. The electronic instrument, which is similar to a television set, shows firing of single neurons. The lower part of the illustration shows the response of a complex-stimuli cell to a moving bar of light. This particular cell responds most strongly to a horizontal bar moving in a downward direction.

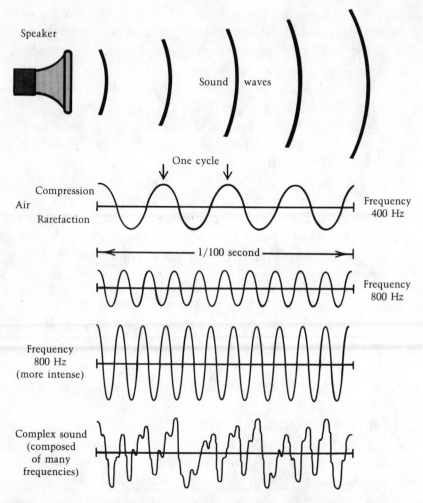

Figure 26 Sound waves formed by compression and rarefaction of the molecules of the air. Shown in the lower part are sound waves varying in frequency and intensity.

second and are characterized by having a *frequency* (or pitch) and *intensity* (or loudness). Frequency is specified in cycles (from compression to rarefaction) per second (you will see this abbreviated CPS or Hz). A young male human can hear frequencies from 20 to 20,000 Hz. With advancing age, high frequency hearing declines. Intensity is rated on a decibel (dB) scale from 0 (the threshold of hearing) to 160 (the level of immediate and permanent damage to the human ear). Figure 27 shows the loudness of common sounds as measured in decibels.

The ear is conveniently divided into three components: external, middle, and inner (Fig. 28). The external ear consists

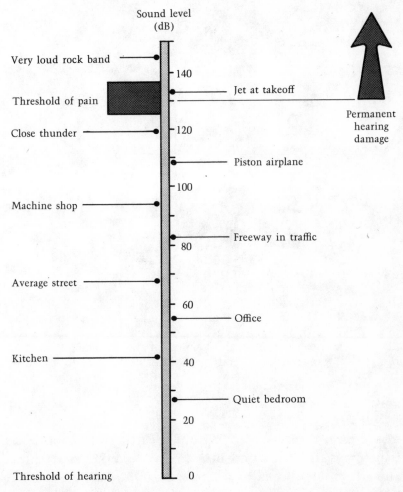

Figure 27 The loudness of various common sounds as measured in decibels.

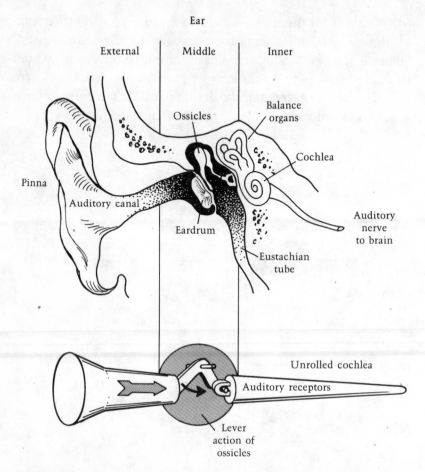

Figure 28 The general structure of the ear. The actual receptor mechanism is in the coiled cochlea. The lower part of the illustration shows a schematic diagram of the ear. The ossicles of the middle ear transmit vibrations from the eardrum into the cochlea.

of the **pinna**, an elaborately formed cartilaginous appendage that serves little function in man, but is quite important in animals more attuned to auditory stimuli. Many animals can move the pinna to a remarkable degree (observe a domestic cat or a German shepherd). In these animals the pinna acts as a "funnel" for sound waves entering the **auditory canal**. The eardrum marks the boundary between the external and middle ear. It is a taut membrane that vibrates at the frequency of the arriving sound waves. These minute vibrations (the smallest are less than one-tenth the diameter of the hydrogen atom) are transmitted to the **cochlea** of the inner ear via the bony **ossicles** of the middle ear. The ossicles, three in number, act as a complicated lever, increasing the force of the vibrations at the expense of their amplitude. The ossicle lever is necessary because the inner ear is filled with fluid, and more force is required to drive the vibrations through the fluid.

The neural receptors for the ear are cells bearing sensory hairs at their apexes. These hair cells are located on the **basilar membrane** in the spiral cochlea of the inner ear. When vibrations are forced through the fluid of the cochlea by the ossicles, the basilar membrane bends toward a second structure, the **tectorial membrane**, which lies on the other side of the hair cells (Fig. 29). This bending causes the sensory hairs to rub against the tectorial membrane, and thus to be stimulated. From the cochlea, the impulses generated by these stimuli travel via the auditory nerve into the brainstem and are relayed to many structures. The auditory nerve terminates in the temporal lobes of the cortex.

The human ear is most sensitive to only a part of the total range of sound waves—namely, the part from 1,000 to 4,000 Hz—the range of the human voice. Other animals have different ranges of greatest sensitivity, coinciding with their ranges of vocalization. Small animals that generally emit high-frequency sounds such as squeaks tend to have the greatest sensitivity for high frequencies. Larger animals that tend to bellow and roar are most sensitive to low frequencies. Each species of animal has a total range of hearing that is somewhat greater than its range of greatest sensitivity, which we have been discussing. These total ranges also differ, of course, from species to species, in the directions that would be expected from consideration of differences in greatest sensitivity.

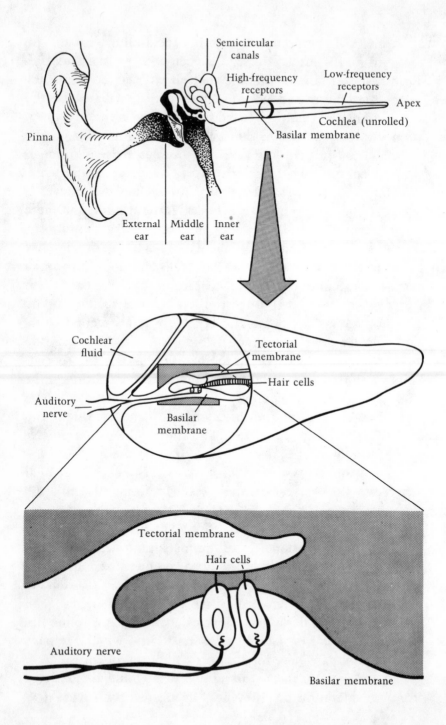

A pure tone (that is, one of single frequency) does not activate the basilar membrane and the tectorial membrane along the entire length of the cochlea, but rather, only a limited area of these membranes begins to vibrate. The locations at which various frequencies cause the membranes to vibrate can be mapped; these are also, of course, the locations of the receptors (the hairs) that generate the corresponding neural impulses. It has been found that receptors for high frequencies are located near the ossicles and those for low frequencies at the far end of the membranes (clearly depicted in Fig. 29 with the cochlea "unrolled"). Thus, hair cells are selectively activated by particular frequencies. Frequencies lower than about 1,000 Hz, however, simultaneously stimulate all hair cells of the human cochlea. In these two ways, the hair cells are able to convey precise information about frequencies to the brain. Most sounds are not pure tones but rather composites of many frequencies; the brain processes the complicated information that results with apparent ease.

The coding of stimulus intensity is the same for all senses: the brain deciphers intensity information from (1) the number of neurons that are active, (2) the rapidity with which they fire, and (3) the activity of special neurons that have a "high threshold," that is, they fire *only* when the stimulus is intense. Auditory pathways are shown in Figure 30; the most powerful input is from the ear on one side of the head to the hemisphere on the opposite side.

Figure 29 A diagram of the ear showing the cochlea "unrolled." The neural receptors are located on the basilar membrane. High frequencies are received near the pinna end of the basilar membrane. Low frequencies are received near the apex. The exploded view of the cochlea shows the tectorial membrane resting on the basilar membrane of the cochlea. The actual sound transduction takes place via hair cells inbedded in the basilar membrane, which are activated by being pressed against the tectorial membrane and send neural impulses out the auditory nerve to the brain.

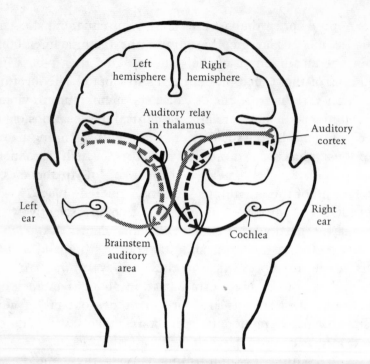

Figure 30 Auditory pathways in the brain. All of these pathways are not crossed (noticed dashed lines), crossed but the most powerful auditory input goes to the opposite hemisphere, that is, right ear to left hemisphere. (Adapted from "The Asymmetry of the Human Brain" by D. Kimura. Copyright © 1973 by Scientific American, Inc. All rights reserved.)

In the region of the cortex specialized for processing auditory information, there is a pattern of areas corresponding to the pattern of receptors on the basilar membrane; that is, the lowest frequencies are processed in the area farthest back, and the highest in the area nearest the front. Thus, the cortex duplicates a representation of the auditory world found in the cochlea. This is a general feature of the senses. You will recall that a representation of the visual world received by the retina is passed on to the visual region of the cortex.

The end result is that the ear is exquisitely sensitive. At the threshold of hearing the ear can detect energy levels equiv-lent to the energy represented by the light from a candle eight miles away. In fact, if the ear were any more sensitive than it is, we would be continually assailed by our own bodily noises—blood pouring through veins and arteries, heart pumping, breath rushing in and out—and by the random bombardment of air molecules against the eardrums. It is possible in a totally soundproof and echo-free room for a person (just barely) to hear these sounds. Normally background noise masks them.

Touch

If I lightly lay my forefinger on your arm, you interpret this as "touch." You also can describe the temperature and texture of my finger. If I press my forefinger into your arm you may report feeling "pressure." If I continue to push down upon your arm, at some point you might cry out in pain. Touch comprises these varied but related sensations. They, as opposed to vision and hearing, do not inform you of distant events, but rather of objects directly touching the body surface. The touch system has a receptor network that tells the brain of the position of the limbs in space and the degree of muscular tension in each muscle. This receptor network will be discussed in detail in a later section.

For many years it was thought that the varied sensations of touch, temperature, texture, pressure, and pain were each detected by specialized receptors in the skin. Such specialized receptors can be identified with the microscope. However, it was shown that a person can experience touch, temperature, and pain from the cornea of the eye—an area that has no specialized receptors but only nonspecialized nerve endings. Specialized receptors in the skin may communicate particular sensations, but they are not necessary for the brain's recognition of the particular sensations, as the cornea experiments show. The body surface is not equally sensitive in all parts to touch, hands and lips being the most sensitive and best equipped to detect small differences in objects. The back and thighs are poorly equipped to detect differences. This is so because the hands and lips have many receptors and the back and thighs have few.

Somatic cortex. We have seen that the visual and auditory receptor systems (retina and cochlea) are "laid out" on the surface of the brain. And, as already described in the introductory discussion of the cortex, the same holds true for the **somatic sensory system** (the touch system). As receptors for touch are located all over the surface of the body, it is not too surprising to learn that the body surface is represented on the surface of the cortex. The body layout on the brain is distorted because the brain allocates cortical space not in terms of anatomical size, but rather in terms of receptor density. As Figure 18 shows, cortical area for the hands and lips of the human is exaggerated in comparison to the physical proportions of these parts, but this "exaggeration" represents their biological importance. Thus such animals as rodents that explore the world largely by sniffing and poking their whisker-rich noses into things have relatively enormous cortical areas for the nose. Similarly, the somatic sensory cortex of tree-living monkeys is largely taken up by areas for fore- and hind-limb digits, which are very important in an arboreal way of life.

If in an experiment a hand area of a human somatic sensory cortex were electrically stimulated, the person serving as the experimental subject would report feeling "something" in the corresponding hand—an ill-defined sensation far removed from the precise sensory information we obtain by merely brushing our fingertips rapidly across an object. Soon, it is hoped, scientists may be able to tell us more about the operation of the touch system.

Kinesthetic Sense

The **kinesthetic sense** is concerned with the orientation and location of the different parts of the body, especially the limbs.

The brain must keep track of the relative position of the parts while the body is engaging in activity. The position of the limbs must be known before they can be moved to a new position and also even to maintain balance when they are not moving. The receptors for the kinesthetic sense are located in the joints, the tendons, and the muscles. We are often consciously unaware of the kinesthetic sense, although we use it continually in our daily activities.

Chemical Senses

The **chemical senses** are smell and taste. The stimuli to which they respond are molecules suspended in either air or liquid. Relatively little is known about the chemical senses, compared to the others, probably because incapacitating damage to these senses is rare, thus reducing a prime motivation to study. Man has a poorly developed sense of smell. Most animals far surpass our rather meager olfactory abilities. In the wild, smell of a predator or prey may be an animal's first cue and one that comes from quite a distance, alerting it long before vision or hearing are effective. In many species, smell is critical for behaviors related to mating, eating, species identification, "family group" identification, and territorial marking.

Taste—at least for the human species—is at once a critical and a relatively unimportant sense. It is critical in the sense that it exerts some control over what a person eats for through his sense of taste he divides foods into **affective categories**; it is likely that a person will eat more of a food to which he has a positive reaction than of one to which his reaction is negative. Taste thus determines our diet to some extent. And, as someone has noted, "you are what you eat." This is quite literally true! Yet taste is relatively unimportant in that much of what we think is taste is actually smell. The classic demonstration is to blindfold someone and plug his nose, give him an onion and a potato to eat, and ask if he can taste the difference. The reply will be "no" and should be

enough to convince even the skeptic. Another large component of "taste" is the activation of pressure receptors in the
mouth (the texture of food is an important determinant of its
palatability), and, with hot, spicy foods, the activation of pain
receptors.

The olfactory receptors are so located in the upper regions
of the nasal cavity that during normal breathing little air
reaches them (Fig. 31). Sniffing changes nasal air flow and
bathes the receptors with the molecules that are in the air.
The neurons leading from these receptors go to an extension
of the brain known as the **olfactory bulb**, which is tiny in
man, but in animals more dependent upon the olfactory sense
is large. The means by which the receptors and olfactory bulb
respond to and code olfactory information remains a mystery.
This is not to say that there are no ideas or theories about the
workings of the olfactory sense; on the contrary, there are a
great many theories. The number of theories explaining a

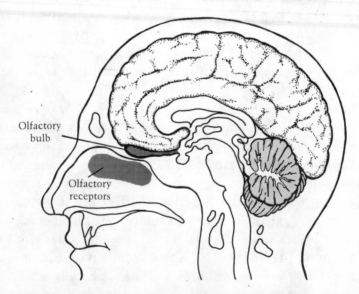

Figure 31 The olfactory brain. The olfactory receptors are located
in the upper portion of the nasal cavity and have neural connections
to the olfactory bulb, which lies below the frontal lobes of the brain.

particular phenomenon may in fact be directly related to the amount of ignorance regarding the phenomenon!

The molecules that we smell are suspended in air. The molecules that we "taste" are suspended in liquid, generally water. Taste receptors are located primarily on the tongue in specialized structures termed **taste buds**. Although we can identify a great number of dissolved substances as each having a unique taste, these can all be expressed as various combinations of four basic tastes: sweet, sour, salty, and bitter.

The sense of taste offers a good example of a principle of brain functioning—adaptation. If we eat mouthful after mouthful of a single food, its taste soon becomes less "strong" or "noticeable." This lessening response is receptor adaptation, a decrease in receptor output during long exposure to a stimulus. The corollary is that the nervous system responds best to change. Coffee tasters have known this for centuries and rinse their mouth with water between tastes in order not only to remove any remainder of the previous sip of coffee but also to maintain the taste receptors in their most sensitive, non-adapted state.

In this section we have examined the senses by which we know the external world. We have seen that the eye is an exquisite little brain in itself, containing several kinds of receptors for black and white and colored light. These receptors contain photochemicals that translate light energy into neural impulses. The visual cortex is so organized—apparently from birth—that it can respond to rather complex visual stimuli without having any prior experience with these stimuli. The ear, too, is a very complex and sensitive structure. The receptors for hearing, found in the cochlea, are hair cells that convert vibrations into neural impulses. From the cochlea information travels to the auditory cortex and "is displayed" upon the cortical surface.

Other sensory systems operate under the same basic rules as do vision and hearing. The touch system is projected onto the somatic cortex in a receptortopic way. Relative areas allotted in the map of the body surface on the cortex express sensitivity of the various body parts rather than their physical size. The kinesthetic sense and the chemical senses also contribute information about the external world.

OUTPUT FROM BRAIN

The most direct agents in the expression of behavior are the muscles of the skeleton. A skeletal muscle, of itself, cannot cause movement. A command comes from the central nervous system via motor neurons in the spinal cord. An action potential from a spinal motor neuron releases transmitter chemical onto the muscle, which then contracts (see pages 22–25). Some of our movements are reflexive and do not require participation of the brain, but all of our voluntary behaviors originate in the brain. The messages are routed out of the brain by the pathways, which end in the spinal cord, of two output systems—the pyramidal system and extrapyramidal system.

Far more is understood about the simpler of the two systems, the **pyramidal system**. It has its origin in the motor area of the frontal cortex where, just as we have described for the somatic cortex, various areas represent various parts of the body. The cortical representation of the body, which has been called a **homunculus**, is roughly that of a prone body stretched along the frontal lobe at the border of the parietal lobe. A homunculus on the right hemisphere represents the left side of the body and one on the left hemisphere represents the right side. Pyramidal-system neurons in the motor cortex have long axons that extend through the brain and deep into the spinal cord. In man these axons are as long as 3 feet and in large whales as long as 30 feet! It is amazing that such cells can even exist. Remember, the nerve cell's machinery, which must look after a lengthy axon, is contained within the cell body.

The **extrapyramidal system** is much more complex than the pyramidal system, and considerably less is known about it. Basically, it consists of many neurons originating deep within the brain in regions under the cortex and having axons that extend into the spinal cord where they interact with the pyramidal axons to produce movement. The pyramidal and extrapyramidal output systems (which we may refer to collectively as the motor system) make extensive use of feedback, a phenomenon familiar to the engineer and encountered in the discussion of biofeedback in a previous section. Biofeedback is purely informational. In contrast, a device may actually be controlled by means of the feeding back into it of the results of its operation. Virtually every home has an example of a feedback device within the heating system of the house—the thermostat. You set the thermostat to warm the house to a particular temperature. The furnace then proceeds to heat the house. When the thermostat detects that the temperature which you designated has been reached, it turns the furnace off until the temperature falls and then the process repeats itself. The motor system uses feedback to compare the actual positions of limbs with the positions to which they are to be moved. The amount and pattern of contraction of the muscles in the limb are determined by continual comparisons of this sort.

The motor system is in full operation even when a person is standing still. The muscles and tendons have receptors that signal the motor system about their state of contraction; the balance receptors in the head signal the motor system about the body's balance and about how weight must be shifted in order to maintain it; receptors of the eyes, the pressure receptors on the bottom of the feet, and receptors that sense the pull of gravity on the limbs all feed signals back to the motor system that assist in the maintenance of upright posture (Fig. 32).

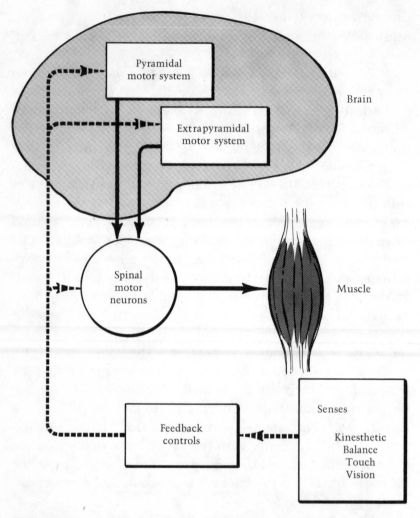

Figure 32 A schematic diagram of the motor systems of the brain connected to the spinal motor neurons and thus to muscle. The motor system of the brain is characterized by extensive use of feedback controls to regulate movements of the organism.

When you undertake a voluntary movement all of these kinds of receptors participate in addition to the brain centers that evaluate the signals in comparison with the desired movement. And miraculously enough, all of this takes place without your giving it much attention.

When you reach for a glass of water you do not consciously think about moving forward four inches and to the side three inches and rotating your wrist 47 degrees and extending your fingers and grasping with enough force to hold the glass firmly without breaking it, and so forth. No—you simply "will it" and it is done! It is almost as if there were a very beautifully designed and executed choreography that was being coordinated expertly by a fine director. The brain sciences cannot, as of yet, explain how these movements are programmed and set into motion by the brain. And yet these are simple movements. Consider the movements made by the accomplished pianist, the rapid typist, the person delivering a speech, the hurdle jumper, or the tennis player.

Electrical stimulation of the human brain has provided insight into the operation of the motor cortex. Pioneering studies showed that stimulation produced movements in a body part corresponding to the portion of the homunculus stimulated. The movements were not jerky twitches; rather they were integrated and directed movements often entailing whole sets of muscles acting in concert. The subjects felt no pain and were often surprised and mildly annoyed at the behavior of, let's say, one of their arms resulting from stimulation. They felt as if the arm were "acting by itself." It was as if they were casual observers of someone else's arm. Indeed, the voluntary control of a subject had no part in the movement; it was produced by the electrical current.

Earlier in this book we examined the muscles and how they contract. We know that muscles do not contract on their own, but rather require impulses from the brain to set them into activity. In this section, we have seen how the brain organizes its output to the muscles. There are two output systems, the pyramidal and the extrapyramidal systems. The origin of these systems is primarily from the motor cortex of the frontal lobe and areas underlying the cortex. The map of the motor cortex is a homunculus very similar to the so-matosensory homunculus. Here too the figure is distorted, expressing the relative precision of movement possible in the various body parts. The motor system of the brain makes extensive use of feedback controls to keep the body operating in a normal and coordinated manner.

BRAIN MOTIVATIONAL SYSTEMS

Why do we eat? Drink? Aspire? Mate? The answers to these questions constitute an area of research concerned with the motivation or causes of behavior. Motivation is not something we can weigh or measure. We see an animal eating and we infer that it is eating because it is hungry. Although such inferences may serve us well for simple behaviors exhibited by "simple" creatures, they may totally fail us when we are observing humans. Consider watching a friend eat lunch. We may assume he is eating lunch because he is hungry. However, we may discover that he is having lunch only because he relishes peanut butter sandwiches. He actually was not hungry at all.

A woman at his table is not eating. Do we infer that she is not hungry? We had better not. She may have forgotten to bring her lunch or her lunch money or perhaps she is on a strict diet and is actually quite hungry. The point is that it is unreliable to infer human motives solely from observed behavior. And we were considering a rather simple behavior. To infer from observed behavior what motivates a person who is going to school, climbing a mountain, or raising a child is tantamount to folly.

Brain scientists are actively trying to provide some measurable underpinning to the quest for the causes of behavior. The search is in the initial phases. It would not be wise to attempt to understand an automobile engine without first understanding levers, gears, and cams. Similarly workers in the neurosciences are trying to understand the causes of simple behaviors in animals rather than complex behaviors in man.

Every animal has needs that must be fulfilled by the environment. These include food, water, air, and a viable range of temperatures. These needs are based on the requirements of tissues and must be met, at least minimally, or the animal will die. The meeting of these requirements ensures (barring biologically nonprogrammed accidents) the survival of the individual *organism*.

Survival of the *species* depends upon successful reproductive behavior, which is usually accompanied by innate or learned social behaviors. One of the functions of social behaviors is to place male and female in proximity, a requisite for mating. The social behaviors can also provide group cohesiveness, protect from danger, and keep a genetic strain pure. All these functions, however, are secondary to the primary goal of reproduction.

We know a great deal about the brain mechanisms resulting in simple behaviors such as eating, drinking, and mating among animals. It is assumed that in time the brain mechanisms underlying more complex behaviors will also be understood. Let us turn to a simple behavior—eating. A basic requirement of an animal is to ingest substances that will meet its tissues' need for an energy source. The question becomes one of how the brain detects the tissues' need for food and how it directs a coordinated series of behaviors that culminate in the ingestion of food.

Eating

It was once thought that animals eat to relieve "hunger pangs," the sensations associated with the contractions of an empty stomach. The logical experiment was to place a balloon in the stomach, inflate it, record changes in air pressure within the balloon as indications of contractions, and compare these "hunger pangs" with the subject's report of being hungry. The initial experiments seemed to disprove the hypothesis that stomach contractions were associated with hunger. What the scientists found was that the balloon showed the stomach to be continually contracting! Later experiments using a somewhat different balloon correctly reported that stomach contractions *were* associated with feelings of hunger. The initial misleading experiment demonstrates a problem often encountered by physicists—that a measuring device may interfere with that which is being measured. In the initial experiments the mere presence of the balloon in the stomach triggered reflex contractions. Such reflex contractions normally follow the arrival of food in the stomach. The problem was resolved by redesigning the balloon to get around the difficulty.

The interference from measuring devices is a serious problem that is often difficult to assess—especially in a human social setting. Another example of such interference comes from an experiment performed in a large industrial plant. In an effort to identify factors that would increase production, the management set up one production line in a special area where they played music, tried various decorating schemes, and so forth. The result of this effort was that production increased remarkably, regardless of what was done. In fact, if nothing was changed from the normal work area, production in the special line was greater anyway! The problem was that the employees knew they were being evaluated when they were working in the special line, and this seems to have motivated them to produce more. Here, too, the measuring device, in the form of the experimental production line, interfered with what the experimenters wished to measure.

To return to our discussion of eating, most of us prefer to eat a hot hamburger rather than a cold one because it tastes better. Thus, it comes as no surprise that taste is a major factor controlling eating. An animal will consistently choose a "good-tasting" diet over a "bad-tasting" one when both contain equal food value. Indeed, one of the principal objections to the projected use of algae farmed from the oceans (which is quite nutritious) is that it does not have a pleasing flavor. Although taste exerts some control over eating, there are other factors operating as well. A rat, for instance, will learn to reject a "good-tasting" food if it subsequently makes him sick. He will also learn to prefer a "bad-tasting" food with nutritive value to a "good-tasting" food that has none.

Some rather fascinating experiments were conducted with small children in relation to taste and eating. The children were allowed to eat all their meals cafeteria style. There were a wide range of foods available, from meats and vegetables to fruits and sweets. The children ate whatever they wished for a period of months. Many mothers would predict that given such a choice children would eat nothing but sweets. They would be only partly correct. The children went on "food jags" during which they would indeed eat vast quantities of sweets. But they would also go on meat jags and vegetable jags. The children were repeatedly examined for any signs of malnutrition, as well as vitamin and mineral deficiency. There were no signs of malnutrition or any dietary deficiencies at the conclusion of the experiment. The children were able somehow to adjust their intake to obtain a completely balanced diet—all without vitamin pills and cajoling mothers! Surprisingly the taste for sweets was overridden by some as yet unknown feedback mechanisms to the brain that directed the children's behavior in selecting more suitable foods.

Let us turn our attention to the means by which tissues receive their energy from the blood. Contained in blood plasma is the sugar glucose. This sugar is utilized by the cells of the body as an energy source. Measurement of blood sugar revealed that when a person feels hunger, his blood sugar level is low. When he is not hungry his blood sugar level is high. A brief look at the condition known as **diabetes** will help clarify the role of blood sugar in eating behavior.

The pancreas gland in a normal person releases a powerful chemical—insulin. This substance enables the tissues of the body to utilize blood sugar. Without insulin blood sugar is not taken into the cells to be used but rather remains in the blood, building up to very high levels. In the diabetic, the pancreas is defective in its production of insulin, resulting in high blood sugar levels (a common means of identifying diabetes) and tissue starvation. If a diabetic is maintained by injections of insulin, he can lead a perfectly normal life. If a person who is not hungry is given a dose of insulin, lowering his blood sugar level, he will experience hunger just as he would if he had gone for some time without eating. Thus, a drop in blood sugar level is a stimulant to eat. Conversely, a high blood sugar level reduces a person's appetite.

This latter effect is the basis for a weight-reducing diet that requires eating a candy bar 30 minutes before meals, the argument being that the increase in blood sugar from eating the candy bar will reduce the appetite at mealtime. Unfortunately for fat people, the inhibitory effects of increased blood sugar are not as effective as the stimulating effects of the presence of food. The "candy-bar diet" is often ineffectual for weight reduction.

Activity pertaining to eating is widespread throughout the brain but that in one region predominates—the hypothalamus (see Fig. 14). The anatomy of the hypothalamus is complex and its interconnections are diverse (see pages 42–43). We will consider only its basic operation. There appear to be two regions of cells within the hypothalamus that are directly concerned with eating behavior. These cells are supplied with information regarding blood sugar level, stomach contractions, taste, and a host of other factors. One of the regions is a "stop eating" center. When a famished rat is electrically stimulated in this region, it ceases eating. The other area is a "start eating" center. A rat that is full will proceed to eat even more when stimulated here. The two centers operate reciprocally, resulting in periods of feeding followed by periods of not eating. The system functions to maintain an adequate level of nutrients in an animal's body. This is an example of **homeostasis**, the maintenance of relatively constant conditions within the body.

The relationship between the two eating centers is one in which they complement one another, yet are diametrically opposed in function, with one center "starting" and the other center "stopping" eating. Such a relationship is also seen in the muscles of the body where one muscle (an extensor such as the triceps) works against another muscle (a flexor such as the biceps) to produce a precise movement. The relationship is termed a *reciprocal* one. Similar relationships are seen elsewhere in the brain.

As you might expect, a rat surgically deprived of its "start eating" center will not eat, even when very hungry and presented with its favorite food. If not force-fed, it will die of starvation. Similarly, a rat missing its "stop eating" center will overeat; in fact, it will continue to eat until it is two or three times its normal weight, and if not stopped will eat itself to death. This animal, although it eats a prodigious amount, is actually quite particular about what it eats. If its food is mixed with bad-tasting substances, the rat will not eat the food. Its hunger seems not to be general, but specific for "good" food. Further, it will not work very hard to obtain its food. A normal hungry rat will perform all sorts of tasks to obtain its ration. Not so for the rat with the hypothalamic "fat rat" syndrome. It will eat copiously only if obtaining the food requires little or no expenditure of its energy.

These observations of the "fat rat" bear a striking similarity to recent research on the "fat man" conducted by S. Schacter. In a series of experiments done quite independently of the brain research on rats, he found that fat men and women eat more than persons whose weight is normal, but only if the food tastes good. Also, in an experiment in which normal and fat subjects were offered nuts in the shell at one time and shelled nuts at another, the fat subjects ate more *only when the nuts were shelled*. This evidence of fat subjects' not being willing to exert much effort to obtain food was corroborated in restaurant observations. It was observed that fat persons tend to choose foods that are easy to eat. For example, roast beef would be preferred over crab in the shell.

In an Oriental restaurant whose customers were all westerners, most fat persons were observed eating with silverware rather than with the more difficult chopsticks.

Laboratory tests showed that although stomach contractions are a reliable indicator of desire to eat in a normal subject, they are not so in the fat man. He is predisposed to eat both in the presence and in the absence of stomach contractions. Apparently the fat man ignores the internal cues that guide the eating behavior of other persons. Schacter hypothesized that the fat subjects were more under the control of external cues like odor and appearance and less under the control of internal events. To test this idea, fat and normal subjects were given the task of proofreading a manuscript for errors. While they were engaged in that task, various disruptions were presented. True to prediction, the fat men were more easily distracted than were the normal men. The suggestion is that fat persons have certain characteristics that both contribute to their overeating and function in behaviors that have nothing to do with eating. On the basis of this, we might suggest the ideal weight-reducing diet for the fat person. The meals would consist of very difficult-to-eat foods served amidst much noise and commotion with the only utensils supplied being chopsticks!

Drinking

An explanation of drinking behavior is very similar to that set forth for eating. An animal's tissues require an external supply of water, and the brain must detect this need and direct behavior for obtaining it. It is also possible for the tissues to be overloaded with water, and the brain must be able to direct elimination of an excess. The human body constantly loses water through breathing, sweating, and the elimination of wastes. This water must be replaced. From eating the body can conserve supplies of food as fat, but bodily reserves of water are scant indeed. A person can go without food for several months, but may die if deprived of water for only several days.

A decrease in body water lowers the amount of stored water surrounding the cells. Water contained in blood is used to replenish these stores. The blood, thus, loses water. The kidneys detect this decrease and secrete a chemical into the blood that is picked up by the hypothalamus. When thus activated, the hypothalamus directs the brain mechanisms that culminate in water-seeking behavior. As for eating behavior, the hypothalamus contains two discrete drinking areas: a "start drinking" area and a "stop drinking" one. Electrical or chemical stimulation of the appropriate center will result in the initiation of the cessation of drinking behavior. Surgical removal or "disconnection" of the appropriate area will produce an animal that will not drink or one that drinks to excess.

Sex

Survival and proliferation of a species depend upon many factors. Examples of two obvious ones are food supply and natural enemies. If, however, a species were incapable of reproducing itself, all the food in the world would not secure its survival. Thus, reproduction has a high rating in the scheme of life. It is no accident that mating behavior or sexual activity is one of the most pleasing and gratifying activities a human can engage in (it may be pleasurable to other animals as well, but such statements are only inferences). After all, if it were unpleasant, people would tend to refrain from sexual activity, which is obviously essential to the existence of the species.

Unlike eating and drinking, sexual activity does not satisfy a tissue need. Although people have been pictured as dying of a broken heart, no one has died as a result of sexual abstinence. Men and women can live quite adequate and full lives without ever engaging in sexual activity. Nonetheless, sexual behavior is a powerful source of human satisfaction and is thus important behavior.

Sexual behavior in man is an enormously complex subject and to deal with it completely would require more space than is available in this book. Therefore, we shall limit our discussion to brain and hormonal influences on sexual behavior and especially to the sexual behavior of laboratory animals. The reader should be aware that research into sexual behavior and the discussion of sex (even from a medical point of view) is a rather recent phenomenon. Sexual activity has been around for quite some time, and people have indeed studied sexual behavior for most of this time. Yet only recently has the study of sex been conducted with less personal interest and more scientific goals and methods.

In most animal species the brain controls and regulates sexual behavior primarily by means of **hormones**. Man and the other primates are notable exceptions to this statement. Man's sexual behavior depends more on personal experience and cultural molding than it does on hormones. A hormone is the chemical product of an **endocrine gland**. There are two general kinds of glands in the body. A gland such as a tear gland or a salivary gland that has a duct delivers its product through the duct to the target site (for example, the surface of the eye or the interior of the mouth). Endocrine glands, which are also called ductless glands, deposit their products—the hormones—into the blood stream. The blood then carries the hormones to every part of the body. A hormone is often described as a substance that carries a "message" through the blood stream. The messages produce specific effects in the activity of cells. Some messages are excitatory and others are inhibitory. Of the two types of behavioral responses—hormonal and neural—the hormonal responses are much slower because they are transmitted by the relatively slow circulatory system. Some hormones such as the growth hormone act upon all of the tissues of the body. Other hormones are specific and cause a reaction in only one organ or at only one location; we call such an organ the target organ of the hormone. The hormonal transport mechanism is much the same as the luggage carrousel in airports. Each suitcase descends from a chute and travels around the carrousel, passing scores of "wrong targets" until its owner snatches it away.

We're discussing the endocrine system in order to understand what regulates sexual behavior. You should, of course, be aware that hormones exert control over many other types of behavior as well. As we shall see, the endocrine system and the nervous system interact so intimately to control sexual behavior that an argument might be made for considering them as parts of a single control system. Such intimate interaction between the two systems also functions in the regulation of the other behaviors that are affected by hormones.

The **pituitary** is the master endocrine gland. It releases a number of hormones each of which performs a different job. The pituitary is termed the master gland because the targets of many of its hormones are other endocrine glands. Table 2 provides a summary of the pituitary hormones, their targets, and their general functions. The mode of operation is relatively simple. The pituitary releases the hormone for a particular gland, which then picks up the hormone from the blood stream and is roused into activity as a result of the

Table 2 The pituitary hormones. Some of these stimulate production of other hormones

Hormone	Target	Effect
Growth hormone	Body tissues	Promotes growth
Thyrotrophic hormone	Thyroid gland	Stimulates production of thyroxin, which regulates metabolic rate
Gonadotrophic hormone	Gonads	Stimulates production of gonadal hormones, which influence secondary sexual characteristics and behavior; regulate pregnancy and birth
Adrenocorticotrophic hormone	Adrenal cortex gland	Stimulates steroid production, which controls water balance, metabolism
Lactogenic hormone	Mammary gland	Stimulates milk production
Oxytocin	Uterus	Stimulates uterine contractions
Vasopressin	Blood vessels	Stimulates vessel contraction; prevents fluid loss

"message" from the pituitary. This gland then produces its own hormone and dumps it into the blood stream where it, too, has a target and an effect. As the second hormone is circulated by the blood to all parts of the body, the pituitary can sense how much of it is being produced, and accordingly reduce or increase its hormone output. This is another example of feedback.

But what does the brain have to do with all of this? What is the "intimate interaction" between the endocrine system and the nervous system? The answer becomes apparent if we ask one more question: What regulates the pituitary?

The hypothalamus, located in the brain directly above the pituitary, is known to exert control over the pituitary by means of neural connections and chemical messengers. Some pituitary hormones are influenced by neural connections, others by chemical messengers. These chemical messengers, hormone-like substances that are called releasing factors, are the means by which the nervous system controls sexual behavior via the endocrine system.

The brain-endocrine control of sexual behavior thus begins when the hypothalamus secretes the appropriate releasing factor into the blood, which quickly reaches the pituitary and stimulates it to secrete **gonadotrophic hormone**. In the female the target gland of the gonadotrophic hormone is the ovary. The ovary has two jobs to perform. First, it produces eggs, and second, it secretes hormones (**estrogen** and **progesterone**). The ovarian hormones make feedback loops to the pituitary, but this is not their sole function by far. Ovarian hormones are responsible for the development of secondary sexual characteristics that superficially distinguish females from males. In the human female such characteristics include the external structure of the genitals, the distribution of body fat and hair, and brain patterns that cause "female-like" responses to certain stimuli.

All mammalian females except the higher primates display cycles in their sexual behavior. These cycles, called **es-**

trous cycles, are due to changes in the relative proportions of the two ovarian hormones. Only during a limited period within the cycle will the female accept the sexual advances of the male. The period of sexual receptivity, called estrus, or heat, is the period during which estrogen increases to its highest level. Sexual behavior in these animals is thus a direct result of a hormonal change. Because the ripening of eggs and their release for possible fertilization is regulated by this same hormonal cycle, the overall effect is to concentrate sexual activity in the period during which the likelihood of conception is greatest.

The human female does not exhibit much cyclical sexual behavior. Ovarian hormones (and eggs) are produced in a regular cycle but this has little effect on behavior. The sexual behavior of human beings is based primarily on past experiences and internalized cultural controls.

In the male the target gland of the gonadotrophic hormone is the testis. Like the ovary, the testis has a dual role: sperm production and hormone production. **Androgens**, the hormones released by the testis, are different from the female hormones, but the general effects are the same. Pituitary hormones stimulate the production of testicular hormones, which, in turn, regulate the production of pituitary hormones by means of feedback. Androgens are also responsible for the development of secondary sexual characteristics and sexual behavior (Fig. 33). In short, there are basic similarities in hormone production in male and female, although the hormones produced are different.

The hypothalamus shapes sexual behavior in another way in addition to its interaction with the endocrine system. In many animals it is the origin of direct neural effects such as mounting behaviors. In this case hormones are not involved.

A good deal is known about sexual behavior and how it is regulated in laboratory animals. Considerably less is known about other animals and man. There is no doubt a good deal of overlap, however. One of the most fruitful ways to consider

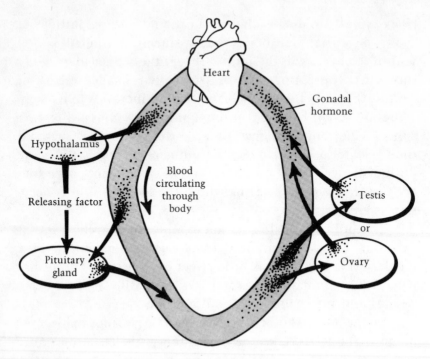

Figure 33 Feedback control of production of gonadal hormones. The hypothalamus causes the pituitary gland to release hormone into the blood that is circulating through the body. This hormone is picked up by the ovary or the testis, which is thereby stimulated to release a gonadal hormone into the blood stream. The gonadal hormone is detected by the pituitary and the hypothalamus, which are thereby inhibited from releasing more pituitary hormone.

the brain-endocrine control of sexual behavior is to examine the effects of various laboratory manipulations on rodents. Rats that are not yet sexually mature do not have appreciable amounts of pituitary hormones circulating in their bloodstreams. As the pituitary hormone is not present, the ovaries or testes of young rats are not active.

If female hormones are administered to an immature male rat, the animal will display adult female sexual behaviors. These behaviors include the retrieval of young and stereotyped female postures. If male hormones are given to an immature male, adult male sex behaviors are observed. Thus, the behavior of the immature rat may be altered by hormones (see Table 3).

Hormonal manipulation has also been attempted on adult animals, whose pituitaries are producing gonadotrophic hormones and whose gonads have developed. Administration of female hormones to an adult male does not produce characteristic female sexual behaviors. In fact, the behavior of the animals does not change much, if at all. If male hormones are administered to an adult male, the result is again minimal. Thus, it appears that once the pituitary comes into play at puberty hormonal injections have little or no effect.

It is known that there is a crucial period in a developing embryo regarding the development of sexual organs. Up to a certain stage mammalian embryos have the capacity to become either male or female depending on pituitary (and in turn brain) activity. Normally, the pituitary hormones are

Table 3 The effects of hormonal treatment upon the sexual behavior of laboratory rats

Subjects	Treatment	Behavior
Immature male rats	None	No sexual behavior
	Give androgens	Adult male sexual behavior
	Give estrogens	Adult female sexual behavior
Mature male rats	None	Adult male sexual behavior
	Give androgens	Adult male sexual behavior
	Give estrogens	Adult male sexual behavior
Mature male rats castrated when immature	None	No sexual behavior
	Give androgens	Adult male sexual behavior
	Give estrogens	Adult female sexual behavior
Mature male rats castrated when mature	None	Gradual decline in adult male sexual behavior
	Give androgens	Maintains or reestablishes adult male sexual behavior
	Give estrogens	Gradual decline in adult male sexual behavior

genetically controlled, and bring about development of the sex that was determined at conception. Pituitary activity can be interfered with experimentally, permitting change in the sex of a developing animal almost at will. After the critical development stage has passed, however, it is impossible to alter the course of sexual development in any major way.

You might expect that if rats were deprived of pituitary hormones throughout their lives, they would be rather asexual. Removal of the pituitary for experimental purposes is not a possibility because it governs so many other vital functions. The next best thing for the investigation we're interested in is to remove the gonads upon which the pituitary acts. A castrated immature rat will not develop sexual behaviors because he has no gonadal hormones. If, however, he is administered male hormones as an adult, he will display adult male sexual behavior. If he is administered female hormones, his behavior will be female. Thus this animal, like the immature rat, has proved to be susceptible to hormonal molding of sexual behavior. If injections of male hormone are given regularly, he can perform the sexual behaviors of a normal male (mounting and so on) but obviously cannot father rat pups because he is lacking in sperm production machinery.

The story for a male rat that is castrated after reaching sexual maturity, is somewhat more complex. His male sexual behavior will slowly decline with time. If, however, he has had a lot of experience in sexual matters, his old behavior patterns may die more slowly than would a rat's who had abstained. The sexual behaviors of a castrated adult can be restored by administration of male hormone. The effect of castration on adult humans is even more dependent upon experience. In fact, it is usually impossible to detect any difference in sexual behavior for years following castration.

Vasectomy, which is simple to perform in humans, is the surgical removal of a part of the vas deferens, the structure that carries the sperm from the testes to the penis. This operation, which is performed as a means of birth control, should not be confused with castration. The testes remain to act as glands, and still respond to pituitary commands to secrete testicular hormones. Thus, possible side effects of castration do not accompany this operation.

In this section we have examined brain mechanisms that control certain behaviors. There are, for example, a number of influences that work together to determine whether an animal will start or stop eating. These influences include stomach contractions, taste of food, and blood sugar level. We have seen that one part of the brain, the hypothalamus, is intimately involved in the regulation of eating behaviors. In fact, there are two special areas within the hypothalamus, one that controls the onset of eating, and one that controls the cessation of eating.

The control of drinking behavior is under similar hypothalamic control. The hypothalamus monitors the amount of water in the body and directs behavior to maintain the required amount.

Sexual behavior is similarly under brain control. In addition to purely neural control, sexual behavior is under the regulation of hormonal influences as well. Particularly with other animals than the primates, the hormonal levels in the blood determine sexual behavior. The pituitary and the hypothalamus interact as a two-part control system, with feedback being an essential mechanism in the system. The physical development of the gonads in both man and lower animals is under the brain-directed control of the pituitary. Once the pituitary establishes control, it is impossible to alter the physical aspect of sexuality or to change sexual behavior appreciably. Injected sex hormones can elicit sexual behavior in rats, but in man, the administration of sex hormones produces less apparent effects because human sexual behavior is determined primarily by past experience rather than by hormonal levels.

SUGGESTIONS FOR FURTHER READING

Eccles, J. The Synapse, *Scientific American*, January 1965. (Offprint 1001)

Evarts, E. V. Brain Mechanisms in Movement, *Scientific American*, July 1973. (Offprint 1277)

Fisher, A. E. Chemical Stimulation of the Brain, *Scientific American*, June 1964. (Offprint 485)

Gregory, R. L. *Eye and Brain*. New York: McGraw-Hill, 1966.

Guillemin, R., and Burgus, R. The Hormones of the Hypothalamus, *Scientific American*, November 1972. (Offprint 1260)

Heimer, L. Pathways in the Brain, *Scientific American*, July 1971. (Offprint 1227)

Hubel, D. H. The Visual Cortex of the Brain, *Scientific American*, November 1963. (Offprint 168)

Kandel, E. R. Nerve Cells and Behavior, *Scientific American*, July 1970. (Offprint 1182)

Katz, B. How Cells Communicate, *Scientific American*, September 1961. (Offprint 98)

Levine, S. Sex Differences in the Brain, *Scientific American*, April 1966. (Offprint 498)

Merton, P. A. How We Control the Contraction of Our Muscles, *Scientific American*, May 1972. (Offprint 1249)

Michael, C. R. Retinal Processing of Visual Images, *Scientific American*, May 1969. (Offprint 1143)

Miller, W. H., Ratliff, F., and Hartline, H. K. How Cells Receive Stimuli, *Scientific American*, September 1961. (Offprint 99)

Pettigrew, J. D. The Neurophysiology of Binocular Vision, *Scientific American*, August 1972. (Offprint 1255)

Pritchard, R. M. Stabilized Images on the Retina, *Scientific American*, June 1961. (Offprint 466)

Stent, G. S. Cellular Communication, *Scientific American*, September 1972. (Offprint 1257)

Thompson, R. F. *Physiological Psychology*. San Francisco: W. H. Freeman and Company, 1972.

von Békésy, G. The Ear, *Scientific American*, August 1957. (Offprint 44)

3

BRAIN AND BEHAVIOR

In this chapter we shall discuss several important topics that are being actively investigated in the brain sciences. Some of the topics concern normal processes that take place in living animals. Others concern external influences that, being brought to bear on the brain, alter it and thus alter behavior also. Some common social problems such as drug abuse are involved among the latter topics. Some of the external influences such as the electrical stimulation of the brain by means of electrodes implanted deep within the brain are rather unusual (except in science fiction).

EARLY EXPERIENCES

In a preceding chapter (pages 58–61), we saw that the visual cortex of a cat's brain was essentially "prewired." The responses of individual neurons in a newborn kitten are similar to those in an adult cat. From this and other evidence it was deduced that much of the brain is ready-to-use and does not depend on experience to make it operative. This does not mean, however, that the environment of an animal or man has no effect on his brain. Far from it—the environment profoundly affects the brain, especially the brain of a growing and developing animal. During its development the brain is most susceptible to change—change that may be brought about by environmental events.

A developing animal must have some contact with the visual world. Without visual experiences the elegant prewiring of the visual cortex will be for nought—the fine and intricate structure will break down and the potential visual ability will deteriorate. We may assume that the same ground rules hold for other brain systems: Direct experience of the environment is necessary for both development and maintenance of the sensory cortex. Thus, although an organism is "given," if you will, a functioning sensory analyzer, he *must* interact with the environment to prevent deterioration of this equipment and to develop its potential to the full. The implication is clear—if you do not use it you will lose it!

Even as deprivation of visual experience can affect the basic neural organization, so can less severe alterations in the environment, although, of course, with less severe effects. A convincing example is provided by experiments in which men wore special goggles that distort vision. The simplest distortion merely displaced the visual field by 5 or 10 degrees (Fig. 34). The effect was that an object at arm's length viewed as being "dead ahead" was actually located 6 or 8 inches to one side. As you might expect, this made it difficult for the wearer to move through space. It took only a few hours' experience, however, for the wearer to become perfectly accustomed to the displacement.

A more drastic distortion was produced by goggles that inverted the visual world. Here too there was an initial period of confusion and disorientation. But after a few days, the wearer was so at ease with his topsy-turvy world that he could successfully navigate a bicycle down a crowded street! So ac-

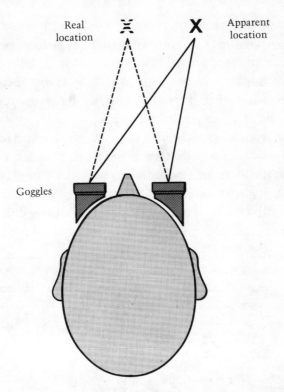

Figure 34 An experiment in which special goggles were worn that visually displaced objects in the environment. The wearers adjusted to minor spatial displacements as well as to a completely upside-down world rather quickly.

customed had the subject become to his upside-down world that when the goggles were removed, and his vision was "normal" again, he reported that the image of the world was upside-down again! Obviously, the human brain is capable of adjusting to such environmental changes as a visual inversion. Not all animals are endowed with such a versatile brain—a newly hatched chick fitted with goggles that displace the visual world will, unlike man, never adjust to the displacement and will continue to peck where it "sees" the grain.

These changes in the brain due to alterations in the visual world caused by wearing the goggles are temporary, short-term solutions devised to meet specific problems. The brain produces other types of solutions that seem to depend upon wired-in, or innate, preferences or aversions, such as fear of depth, that apparently function throughout life. Experiments using the **visual cliff** have demonstrated the universality of this aversion. If a human infant is placed on an apparatus like the one in Figure 35, which has a thick glass surface with a patterned design immediately beneath the glass on one side and the same pattern several feet beneath the glass on the other side, he will consistently avoid the "deep" side. Also, animals as diverse as lambs, chicks, and human children will

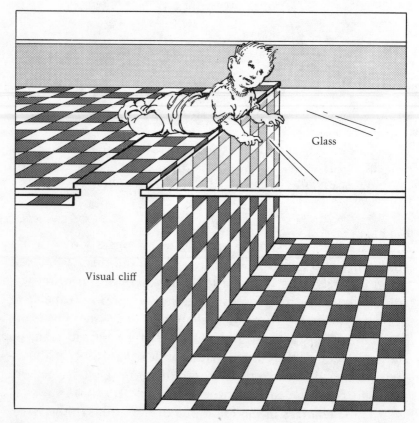

Figure 35 The visual cliff.

scurry out of the "deep" side if placed on the glass over it, even though they can feel the solid glass under their bodies!

In recent experiments adult cats that had been reared either in an environment enclosed by a surface on which were painted horizontal stripes or in one with vertical stripes were tested for evidences of permanent alteration in the visual region of the brain. The results were clear. Neurons in the visual cortex of cats reared with the vertical stripes responded far better to vertical than to horizontal images. Similarly, cats reared with the horizontal stripes had neurons that responded far better to horizontal than to vertical images.

The results of these experiments are quite illuminating: they suggest that man can, through manipulation of the environment, alter the brain itself. Nevertheless, we cannot be sure that the matter of the brain was actually altered in the sense of having one kind of patterning in it replaced by another. It could be, for example, that neurons in the "vertical" cats that normally respond to horizontality have died rather than being transformed into neurons that respond to verticality.

We have seen that the brain is a complex structure whose blueprint is laid down in the genetic code of an animal. This is not to say that the environment has no effect on the developing brain or on its ultimate function. Indeed, the environment plays a great role in determining both the nature of the brain and behavior. In this section we have seen several examples of how the environment profoundly affects the brain. Environmental effects are especially pronounced on a developing brain. Many experiments have shown that interactions of the environment with the brain can produce profound changes in brain function itself. In summary, we can say that although an animal inherits a brain based on a genetic blueprint, its final form and function is determined by interactions with the environment.

NATURE-NURTURE

For many years it was alternately fashionable to argue that the major determinant of a child's personality was (1) innate (the *nature argument*) or (2) learned (the *nurture argument*). These approaches ignored the fact that neither innate nor learned factors operate upon development in a vacuum. Each requires the other. The only reasonable question is "what is the interaction between nature and nurture?" A logical means of investigating this question is to hold nature constant and vary nurture. A difficulty arises in holding nature constant, however, in studies of human beings—controlled breeding experiments are not a possibility! It is therefore helpful to use other animals in experiments designed to determine the general principles governing the interaction between nature and nurture. The laboratory rat, which has been inbred for many generations, is a particularly good subject for such experiments because a great deal is known about its genetic history.

In a series of experiments conducted at the University of California, Berkeley, brain scientists constructed an elaborate "kindergarten" for laboratory rats (Fig. 36). The purpose was to answer the critical question of the degree to which the environment can interact with and alter the basic structure of the brain. The strategy employed is to provide rats that are littermates with varying degrees of "environmental enrichment." Some of the littermates were kept socially isolated, that is, one to a cage with the cages far enough apart to prevent social interaction. This group of rats was what scientists call an **experimental control group**. From measurements made on these rats the experimenters obtained standards to be used in comparisons to judge what effects enriching the environment had on the other rats. The "enrichment" comprised social interaction with their peers plus the availability of toys carefully chosen to gladden the heart of any young rat. On reaching a certain age the rats were given the rat equivalent of an IQ test. Upon close examination it was discovered that rats

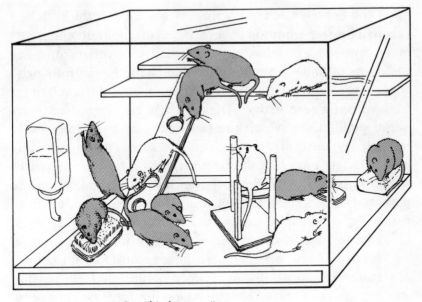

Rat "kindergarten"

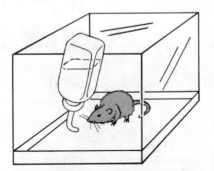

Impoverished environment

Figure 36 Living in an enriched environment.

from an enriched environment had a markedly "superior" brain as determined by a number of measures. The cortex of the "enriched" rats was thicker, suggesting that the neurons, which had not increased in number, had formed a more complex net of interconnections.

The Berkeley scientists also discovered that the enriched rats had greater amounts of several important brain chemicals and surpassed the other rats according to a variety of other measures of brain growth and development. Not surprisingly, these rats also did better on the IQ test than did the relatively impoverished littermates. The test was a discrimination reversal problem for which the rats had to reverse a previously learned response of approaching one stimulus and avoiding another. The enriched animals performed much better than their "impoverished" peers. These studies demonstrated the potential of the brain to grow and develop in a rich environment. They were used in a successful campaign for enactment of social legislation to aid the children of the disadvantaged.

Harry Harlow, a scientist at the University of Wisconsin, also studied the relationship between nature and nurture—not in the context of brain growth and environmental complexity, but rather in regard to the factors governing "mother love." Harlow's experimental subjects were monkeys. For some time it had been fashionable to consider that the affection for mother readily exhibited by man and many animals was due to a learned dependency. That is, a helpless infant received life-giving food from its mother and thus was positively reinforced by the alleviation of hunger for approaching and clinging to its mother. This view was dealt a deathblow by the work of Harlow.

What Harlow did was to capitalize on the observation that infant monkeys become very attached to pieces of cloth placed in their cages. They become acutely distressed if their "Linus blankets" are removed even for short periods. Harlow theorized, correctly as we shall see later, that physical contact was a prime moving force in the development of the mother–child bond of affection. The experiment used two groups of infant monkeys. Each of the monkeys was placed in a special cage that contained two *"surrogate" mothers*. One of the surrogate mothers, as shown in Figure 37, was constructed of bare wire and the other of wire covered with soft terrycloth. De-

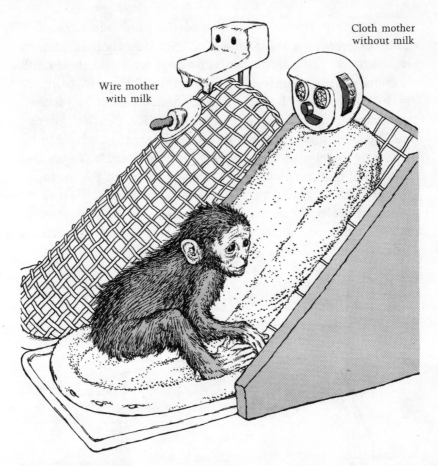

Wire mother
with milk

Cloth mother
without milk

Figure 37 Cloth and wire surrogate mothers.

pending upon which group an infant monkey was in, he received his milk from a nipple protruding from either the wire or cloth mother's "breast." Harlow simply noted which of the two surrogate mothers the infants spent time with. Those people favoring a learned-dependency explanation of mother love would, of course, predict that the monkeys would prefer whichever surrogate mother supplied them with milk. However, had these persons wagered on the outcome of the experiment they would have emerged poorer. All of the monkeys, as is shown in Figure 38, preferred the cloth mothers, *even those that received their milk from the wire mother*. Harlow termed the binding force between the infants and their cloth mothers **contact comfort**. To paraphrase Harlow concerning the controversy: If learned dependencies are to be invoked as an explanation of the monkeys' behavior, the dependency must be fashioned from whole cloth rather than whole milk.

Harlow went on to show that other factors also enter into an infant's preference among surrogate mothers. For example, a warm cloth mother is preferred over a cool one and a rocking mother is preferred over a still one. That the infant monkeys really felt that the surrogates were mothers was demonstrated

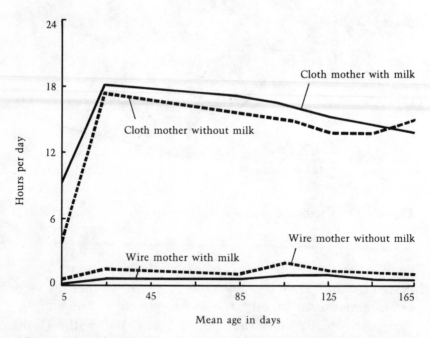

Figure 38 The amount of time infant monkeys spent with the cloth mother or with the wire mother. The presence or absence of food associated with the surrogate mothers made little difference in the animals' behavior toward them. (Adapted from "Love in Infant Monkeys" by H. F. Harlow. Copyright © 1959 by Scientific American, Inc. All rights reserved.)

rather convincingly by a variety of further demonstrations. At one point the infants were placed into small rooms that had in them objects, such as rattles, plastic "creatures," and other children's toys, that seemed to be frightening to the monkeys. If the surrogate mothers were also in the room the infant would immediately rush to the cloth mother for protection and comfort. Only after clinging for awhile to the cloth surrogate would the infant begin to explore the new territory.

If, however, the cloth mother was absent from the room the infant would freeze in terror and howl until removed. Thus, we can see that contact comfort, at least for the monkey, is the most important determinant in his recognition of a "mother."

The brain is an exquisitely complex organ. This complexity is determined partly by genetic inheritance and partly by interactions with the environment. Behavior, in turn, is under the control of the brain and thus shaped by both nature and nurture. Scientists are now beginning to unravel the brain mechanisms underlying behavior. It can be expected that in the years to come neuroscientists will understand more clearly the interplay between the two components. The identification of genetic and environmental influences on brain function (and thus on behavior) may allow us to eliminate negative influences and enhance positive ones. Such knowledge, properly applied, might do much to improve the human condition.

In this section we examined the nature–nurture issue and saw that the important question is, what is the interaction between nature and nurture? Although it is easy to pose the question in this manner, it is not necessarily easy to do the appropriate experiments to answer it because genetic and environmental factors cannot always be controlled. Several strategies have been reviewed here, including the use of the inbred laboratory rat. It was shown that laboratory rats exposed to an enriched environment actually develop changes in the basic structure of the brain. The nature–nurture question was viewed from the aspect of mother—child relationships in monkeys. For a long time, it had been believed that the bond between mother and child was formed as a result of the infant's receiving nourishment from the mother. The experiments with monkeys invalidated this belief. They showed that the receipt of food from a "mother" was not the important factor in determining an infant's attachment to her. Rather the provision of a soft surface to which the infant could cling was the important factor.

ELECTRICAL ACTIVITY OF THE BRAIN

The brain is *not* an electric machine; it does not run on electricity, nor does it generate much electricity (something on the order of a few millionths of a volt at the surface of the brain). It is a biochemical machine; it runs on metabolic substances and conducts its business by electrochemical means (see pages 26–31). Nevertheless, the electricity generated as a byproduct of the electrochemical events can be measured and the measurements so obtained permit scientists to examine the more basic electrochemistry. A physician doesn't often open the chest to observe the heart; he relies upon listening to the heart sounds with a stethoscope. He has learned that the various sounds signify different events and conditions. Analogously, the brain scientist has learned about the relations between a recording of the electrical activity in the brain and the underlying electrochemical events.

There are two ways to record the electrical activity of the brain. The first and most common is to place metal disc electrodes on the surface of the scalp and record the electrical activity of the brain beneath. The very weak signals are amplified and recorded on a moving paper. The graphic record is an **electroencephalogram** (EEG). Figure 39 shows a schematic

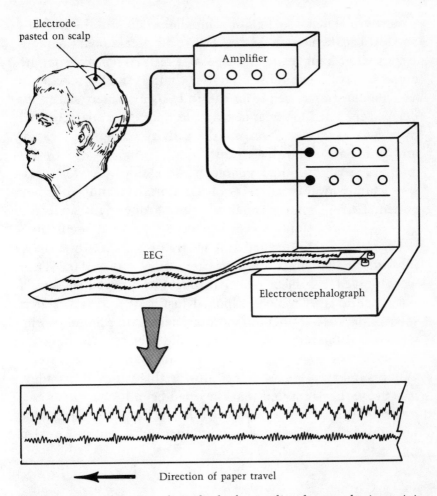

Figure 39 The general method of recording human brain activity. Activity is picked up by electrodes on the scalp, amplified, and written out on a moving paper by a electroencephalograph. This records the changing voltage generated by the brain over time.

of the recording instrument, which is called an electroencephalograph. Electrodes can be placed over many different brain areas and an EEG can then be made of the activity of countless millions of brain cells acting, more or less, together.

To the uninitiated the EEG appears to be a meaningless collection of squiggly lines. However, study reveals consistent patterns in EEGs and relationships between certain patterns and various behavioral states. Figure 40 dramatically demonstrates what happens to the EEG of a relaxed person when he closes his eyes. The most profound changes in EEG take place as a person progresses from the fully awake, alert state into deep sleep. The EEG of an awake, alert person is characterized by a general lack of "waves," the activity being slight, rapid, and irregular as shown in Figure 41.

There is a different characteristic EEG pattern for a person who is awake but relaxed, comfortable, and with eyes closed. During relaxed wakefulness the dominant wave frequency recorded on an EEG is between 8 and 12 oscillations per second—this is termed **alpha activity**. The EEG of a sleeping subject is characterized by large, slow waves (Fig. 41). If we observed a subject's EEG throughout a night we would notice periods in which it looked just as it did during alert wakefulness. This phenomenon puzzled brain scientists, who named it paradoxical sleep because the subject is sleeping but his brain waves resemble those of an alert, awake person. When subjects were awakened during this period of paradoxical sleep, they reported that they had been in the throes of a dream. Thus, the EEG made while the subject is dreaming resembles that of an awake individual! Observation revealed

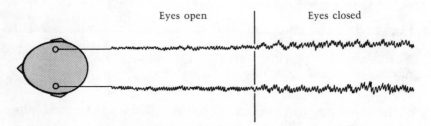

Eyes open | Eyes closed

Figure 40 EEGs showing the transition from eyes open to eyes closed in a resting human being. A characteristic "signature" is obtained with eyes closed. (Adapted from "The Electrical Activity of the Brain" by W. G. Walter. Copyright © 1954 by Scientific American, Inc. All rights reserved.)

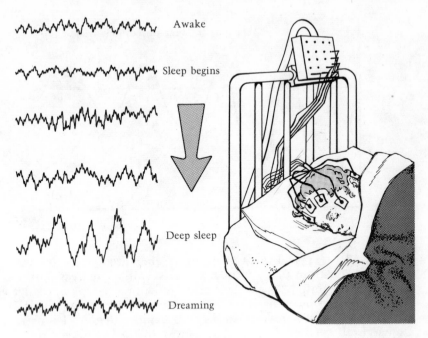

Figure 41 Typical EEGs from subjects in different states ranging from alert wakefulness to dreaming.

that the eyes dart to and fro during dreams, giving rise to the term rapid-eye-movement (**REM**) sleep to describe the dreaming state.

Apparently we all dream, although some of us are better at recalling dreams than others. Experiments have shown that even persons who claim they "never dream" actually do, although not as often as other people. They apparently forget the dreams they do have. The "average dreamer" has five to seven per night with each dream lasting from 10 to 40 minutes. Dreams get longer as the night progresses (Fig. 42). Contrary to popular belief, we dream in "real time," not in super-fast or super-slow time. Many people dream in color and stereophonic sound! Most of us are unaware of the subject matter of most of our dreams. We generally remember a dream best if we are awakened in the midst of it. In detailed studies of

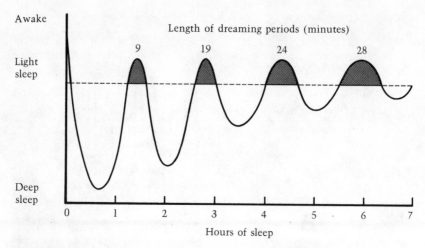

Figure 42 A typical night of sleep—a generalized graph based on all-night EEGs from many human subjects. Darkened areas indicate periods of dreaming. As can be seen, the depth of sleep progressively declines toward morning and the length of the dreaming periods increases. (Adapted from "Patterns of Dreaming" by N. Kleitman. Copyright © 1960 by Scientific American, Inc. All rights reserved.)

dream content hundreds of people were queried about the contents of thousands of dreams. The picture that emerges is that novelty has a predominant role in dreams. A third of dream time is spent merely in going away from or toward something. A high proportion of dream time is taken up by active sports and a low proportion by dull routine. People report that the dreams following a rather dull day are sometimes spectacular and exciting, whereas the dreams following a day full of invigorating activities tend to be bland and tame. It is almost as if a dream were compensating for daily activity.

REM sleep is not limited to adults; it has been observed in newborn infants and many animals. A sleeping dog or cat can be observed to move his eyes rapidly, perhaps move his limbs, and vocalize. The animal is exhibiting that it is in REM sleep, and although we cannot confirm it, is almost certainly dreaming. The obvious question is, "What does a newborn baby or a dog dream about?" Unfortunately, we cannot answer this question directly. A partial answer is provided by experiments, on both man and animals, in which REM sleep was interrupted. That is, every time a subject went into REM sleep he was awakened, and thus deprived of the normal amount of dreaming. The results of the experiments were that the humans became very irritable and showed signs of mental disturbances. The symptoms disappeared following a night of uninterrupted sleep. Interestingly, the subjects, both animal and human, tended to "make up" lost REM sleep time on subsequent nights, when they exhibited evidence of half again as much REM activity as normal. An unfortunate aside is that many sleeping pills contain substances that prevent or reduce REM sleep. Thus, although an individual takes a sleeping pill to obtain a good night's sleep, presumably, he in fact experiences a reduction in his essential REM time and as a result may be worse off than originally.

We have seen that alpha activity is generally seen during relaxed wakefulness. This state is further characterized by feelings of contentment and ease. The pressures of urban life today are such that many people are looking for ways in which to cultivate feelings of peace and contentment. One such approach to this goal is for a person to train himself by using feedback techniques to produce alpha waves. The procedure is simple. An EEG electrode is pasted to the scalp. The weak signal is amplified and put into an electronic device that "recognizes" alpha activity. When alpha waves are detected, a beeping tone sounds or a light flashes. By using this information a person can train himself to do those things that generate alpha activity. There are currently many members of what has been called the "alpha cult." Admittedly many people try alpha training, and as with any other fad, subsequently drop it. But for some it seems to be a satisfying means of achieving a personal goal.

Scientists are fascinated by the concept that a person can so regulate his internal states as to produce changes in alpha activity or blood pressure by using biofeedback. This technique promises much in terms of relief from certain medical disorders such as high blood pressure (see pages 9–15).

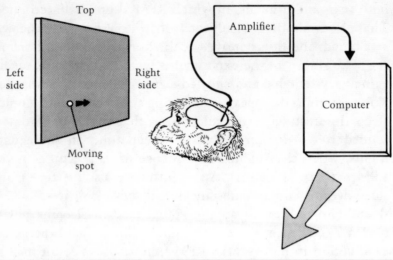

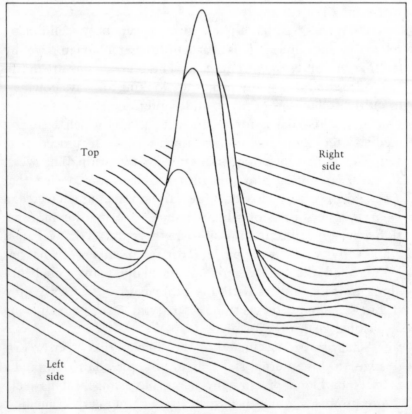

The second method of recording the electrical activity of the brain is almost exclusively limited to the study of the central nervous system in laboratory animals. The electrical activity of single neurons or small numbers of neurons can be recorded by fine-tipped electrodes placed close to the particular cells. Figure 43 shows an experiment done by Karl Pribram in which the responses of single neurons in the visual cortex of monkeys are processed by computer into three dimensional maps. The major advantage of this procedure is that it allows the brain scientist to specify more precisely from what area he is recording electrical activity and to study individual neurons rather than a mass of millions of cells as with the EEG.

Much of our detailed knowledge of the nervous system has come from experiments investigating the function of single neurons. The visual experiments mentioned on pages 58–61 employed single neuron recordings from the cortex of a cat's brain. Experiments more basic to the understanding of how a neuron produces an action potential and responds to synaptic input have used fine electrodes inserted into living neurons. Such intracellular recordings have added to our present knowledge regarding the neural mechanisms responsible for color vision, hearing, and simple forms of learning, to name only a few. The brain is an assemblage of billions of neurons that act together. By understanding the activity of single neurons we can begin to appreciate the operation of the entire brain.

Figure 43 The response of a single neuron in the visual cortex of a monkey. The animal is watching a moving spot while a computer records and plots the visual receptive field map in three dimensions (lower part of illustration). For this particular neuron, the unit fired most when the spot was in the center of the animal's visual field. (Adapted from "The Neurophysiology of Remembering" by K. H. Pribram. Copyright © 1969 by Scientific American, Inc. All rights reserved.)

The electrical activity of the brain can be detected by two means. Surface recording of brain activity, which produces the EEG, has shown us that patterns of brain activity change dramatically as a person moves from one to another of the different states of wakefulness and sleep. Studies of EEGs of sleeping subjects have shown the somewhat surprising fact that when a person is dreaming his EEG resembles that recorded during alert wakefulness. Periods of dreaming are associated with rapid eye movements (REM) in many species. Other behavioral states produce characteristic EEG patterns. An example is the alpha wave associated with relaxed wakefulness. A technique for studying brain activity, which is generally not used in humans, is the recording of brain activity from electrodes inserted directly into the tissues of the central nervous system. Experiments using this technique have provided us with much information regarding brain mechanisms underlying sensation, perception, and action.

ELECTRICAL STIMULATION OF THE BRAIN

We encountered electrical stimulation of the brain in the section in which we saw that weak electric current applied to the motor cortex results in movement of some part of the body. Regions of the brain other than the motor cortex have been stimulated both in man and in animals. The most dramatic examples can be drawn from the medical treatment of persons afflicted with brain tumors. Many brain tumors must be surgically removed to prevent their causing the death of the patient. Brain surgery is delicate, for the central nervous system is very fragile and can easily be damaged. The tumors themselves increase the difficulty, as many of them are buried beneath healthy brain tissue. To minimize damage to the healthy, overlying brain, the neurosurgeon may electrically stimulate regions of the cortex and other areas to determine their precise functions and thus be able to select areas for incision that have less crucial functions. In the course of these procedures a great deal has been learned about brain functioning because the patients are often under only local anesthetic, and thus, can tell what they are experiencing as a result of the electrical stimulation.

As you might expect, the effect of brain stimulation depends upon what area of the brain is stimulated. Since stimulation of the motor area was seen to produce movement, it should come as no surprise that stimulation of the visual cortex gives rise to the experience of light. Not "visions" or "scenes" but rather flashes of light. Similarly, stimulation of the somatic cortex produces sensations of touch or pressure, and activation of the auditory cortex produces the effects of sounds. We take these facts for granted today, but in years past the discovery of this aspect of brain functioning startled many people. The reason is simple: if our brain "tells us" of something in the environment, we have a tendency to believe it—*even if it doesn't exist in the physical world.* In other words, the only way we have of knowing the world is through our brain and sensory receptors.

At one time or another most of us have heard or seen something when in fact nothing was there. The heavy drinker may "see" bugs and snakes crawling over his bed—when, of course, they exist only in his alcohol-steeped brain. The person afflicted with mental illness may "hear" voices talking to him—yet they are not available for anyone else to hear. The point is this: to the person having the hallucinations, they are real, and often frightening.

If our sensory receptors and brain distort the world or create an alternative one, we nevertheless feel that we are receiving information about the real world. We ought not to feel that only alcoholics and the mentally ill experience such delusions: most of us hallucinate rather vividly each night in our dreams. Needless to say, a dream can be a vivid, exciting, terrifying, and "real" experience—yet it is created in the brain.

Figure 44 Dreaming. (Adapted from "What People Dream About" by C. S. Hall. Copyright © 1951 by Scientific American, Inc. All rights reserved.)

If stimulating electrodes are placed over various areas of the cortex, and particularly over the association cortex, a subject may report hearing music, voices, familiar sounds, or he may recall past events that had been long forgotten. By some means the electrical stimulation is drawing a buried memory out of the brain's coffer. If the stimulation is removed the memory wanes but it returns if the stimulation is resumed. It is almost as if a phonograph needle were being repeatedly placed in the same groove of a recording. Surprisingly, if a location giving rise to a specific memory is removed, the memory is not necessarily destroyed. Obviously we cannot assume that the spot was the repository of that memory if recall is possible following surgical removal. This suggests, on the one hand, that memories and functions are localized to a discrete brain location but, on the other hand, that removal of the area does not seriously impair memory or function. This paradox is not limited to association areas and is a formidable barrier to our increased understanding of the brain.

In the 1950's a discovery was made known that startled the scientific world. James Olds reported that after placing stimulating electrodes deep into the brains of rats he could train them in a variety of tasks, *the only reward being the electrical stimulation of their brains.* In fact, the rats would press a lever as rapidly as they could for periods of hours, forgoing food and receptive mates, all to keep the electrical stimulations coming (see Fig. 45). The regions of the brain eliciting these behaviors are certain structures in the limbic system and a part of the hypothalamus, which, as we have seen, is a major integrating system in the brain (see pages 42–43). When corresponding areas in the brain of man are stimulated, the results are similar. People find it difficult to find words to describe the sensation, but report that they like it and would like to continue receiving it.

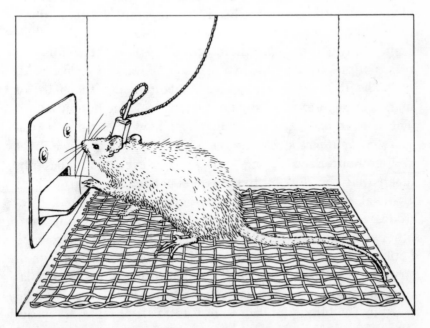

Figure 45 A rat in a Skinner box repeatedly pressing a bar, which causes an electrical stimulations to be delivered to his brain.

The electrical stimulation of other areas of the brain produces diverse results. Stimulation of a region of the limbic system of a cat's brain provokes responses of anger. The animal hisses, arches its back, and seems quite fierce. The rage is only apparent however. While the animal is exhibiting this behavior a person can quite safely pet it. The phenomenon has been given the name "sham rage" because it is machinelike behavior. The animal is not *really* in a state of rage; the electrical stimulation merely produces behavior that is identical to that of rage.

Even more striking experiments have been performed with chickens wearing implanted brain electrodes. When brainstem structures were electrically stimulated in these birds, they performed very complex tasks. The elicited behaviors related to feeding and were very stereotyped. Each time a stimulus was given, the chicken would begin a long string of food-seeking or feeding behaviors that was totally out of context with its ongoing behavior. Apparently these animals have chains of behavior that are "programmed" into their brains. Given an appropriate stimulus these behaviors are reeled off much the same as a movie, one frame after the next.

The thought of electrodes implanted into the brain of man is enough to thrill the heart of any science fiction writer. The picture of a man controlled by a mad scientist or a runaway computer is a bit extreme, even in an age of space flight and computerized dating services; however, that does not mean that the possibilities, both beneficial and harmful, of artificial stimulation of human brains can be ignored. Electrodes are today being worn by a few people suffering from otherwise uncontrollable epileptic seizures. The science fiction novel *The Terminal Man*, by Michael Crichton, when stripped of its drama, is a realistic application of brain stimulation in man. In the not-too-distant future electrodes may be worn by the blind and deaf to restore a part of their lost capacities. Nevertheless, the control of man by means of "applied brain science" seems quite a way off into the future, if indeed it is *ever* possible. There are very good reasons for believing that the brain is an organ of such incredible complexity that the implantation of a number of electrodes could never begin to control its operation. In any event, the entire question of man controlling man is to a large degree academic, for we are all molded by our society, parents, schooling, job, inherited and acquired status, to mention only a few. These control us in ways so effective as to quicken the pulse of any psychologist. Contrasted with these sources of control, which have been perfected over thousands of years by trial and error, any eventual attempt to control man on the part of a neuroscientist may seem feeble by comparison.

We know the world about us only through the activity of our brain. Artificial stimulation of the brain with electrical current can produce sensations normally provoked only by stimuli received from the environment. Muscles can be made to move by stimulation of the motor areas of the brain. Stimulating electrodes placed in the association areas of the brain often evoke vivid memories of past events.

Some areas of the brain respond to electrical stimulation by producing set patterns of behavior, such as sham rage. Stimulation of certain areas of the brain produces sensations that may act as powerful positive or negative reinforcers in instrumental learning and thus can be employed to motivate animals to perform a complex series of behaviors. There are some peculiarly human implications that must be taken into account in considerations of artificial stimulation of the brain of man.

LANGUAGE AND THE BRAIN

The possession of complex language is unique to man. It is true that animals communicate. Their communication is, however, crude in comparison with man's. Many lower animals convey information from one to another by means of secreted chemicals that have certain odors. Higher animals usually communicate with their vocal apparatuses. What animals communicate is open to speculation. It is generally agreed, however, that they communicate emotions and information directly related to survival (about danger, food, and so forth). Only man has formal language, which has rules of syntax.

All languages known to man have similar deep structures. Only the surface structures differ. Although the sounds of each language are somewhat unique there are about 40 identifiable sounds in any language. These observations among others have led many to propose that man is innately equipped with the capacity for language. In accord with this reasoning, it may further be explained that the environment merely shapes the biological underpinning of language into a particular mode of expression, be it English, Spanish or Slavic.

The notion of language being innate to man is, at the moment, an issue of hot debate. There are precedents to show that many complex functions are handled by genetically wired brain circuits. We discussed some relevant experiments carried out by Hubel and Wiesel on pages 59–61. Thus, it is not inconceivable that the brain is prewired with some basic equipment for language development.

Most of the information we possess regarding brain involvement in language comes from persons suffering from brain damage. The language deficits resulting from brain damage are known as **aphasias**. The kinds of brain damage resulting in aphasia are fairly well known. Tumors or penetrating head wounds that damage either of two cortical locations —Broca's and Wernicke's areas—in a person's dominant hemisphere (Fig. 46) are very likely to cause aphasia, which may take one of several forms.

The results of hundreds of case studies have suggested that Broca's area is responsible for the "output processing" of language, or more precisely, that it contains the rules by which

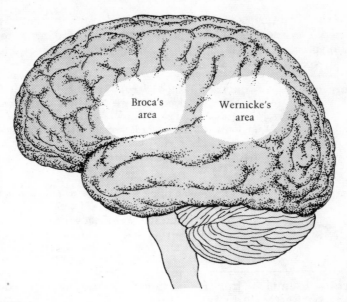

Figure 46 Speech areas of the cortex in the dominant hemisphere of the human brain.

a speaker codes his ideas into language. Damage to Broca's area produces speech made up of intelligible words that do not relate to each other coherently (Table 4). Wernicke's area, on the other hand, seems to operate in "input processing," or the comprehension of the language of others. These effects are seen only if the damage is in the dominant hemisphere. In a right-handed person the dominant hemisphere is the left. Aphasia in an adult is almost certainly permanent, but a child suffering from aphasia may completely recover if the other side of his brain is undamaged. Apparently the brain of a child is sufficiently adaptable to compensate for damage to a part of it.

Electrical recording from the scalp overlying the cortical language areas has shown that brain potentials evoked by words are more pronounced over the dominant hemisphere. This is in accord with the clinical findings of the effects of brain damage to the dominant hemisphere.

Table 4 Transcripts of the speech of persons suffering from aphasias. The speaker in example A had suffered damage to the anterior speech cortex (Broca's area); the speaker in B, damage to the posterior speech cortex (Wernicke's area).

Example A	I am taking—ah—Sherriks—ah—Sherring's mixture (laugh). It's easier for me to—stalk—talk staccato and breaking up each word—into sentences—breaking up sentences into words provided they have ah—not many syllables. Ah, syllable is hard—. Precise words that I have trouble with are Republican and Epics—Epis—capalian.
Example B	Well, I thought thing I am going to tell is about my operation and it is not about all I can tell is about the preparation the had was already the time was when they had me to get ready that is they shaved off all my hair was and a few odd parts of pencil they give me in the fanny.

Sources: Example A from E. G. Lenneberg, *Biological Foundations of Language*, New York: Wiley, 1967, p. 195; example B from W. Penfield and L. Roberts, *Speech and Brain Mechanisms*, Princeton, N.J.: Princeton University Press, 1959.

Interesting experiments have been performed that claim to show differences in brain activity that are associated with word meaning. In such experiments the subjects hear a single word that can be interpreted two ways, that is, an ambiguous word. The brain activity from language centers of the cortex shows marked differences depending upon which of the two meanings is perceived (Fig. 47).

There are two cortical areas of the brain that appear to be specialized for language. One is for the input processing of language and the other for the output processing. Much of our knowledge of the functions of these areas has come from persons whose brains have been damaged in one or both of these areas. Electrical recording of brain activity has contributed to our knowledge of brain processes in language.

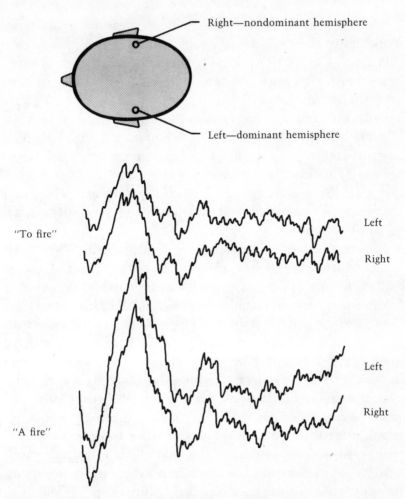

Figure 47 An experiment showing different brain activity in response to the word "fire" depending on whether it is interpreted as a verb ("to fire") or a noun ("a fire). The lines shown were obtained by taking the algebraic average of many individual EEGs from the language cortex on the left hemisphere and from an analogous location on the right hemisphere.

CONSCIOUSNESS AND AWARENESS

Psychology has been defined as the study of consciousness. By this is meant the mental life of an individual—feelings, sensations, thoughts, and whatever else it is that goes on within our skulls every day. The brain scientist cannot explain the workings of the "mind" . . . yet. The sum total of our consciousness—of our "mind"—is the product of very complicated brain processes. We are only now beginning to learn how the brain works in performing simple tasks such as responding to sensory information and generating movement. The brain scientist is still at a loss when it comes to explaining desires, ambitions, or other feelings in terms of brain mechanisms. This does not mean that these feelings are not the result of brain activity—they most certainly are. The brain mechanisms associated with them are simply poorly understood at this time.

Considerable progress in our understanding has been achieved by studying humans afflicted with various brain disorders. Roger Sperry has provided a dramatic demonstration of the differences in function between the dominant and nondominant hemispheres. His subjects were several neurosurgical patients whose two hemispheres had been surgically disconnected as a treatment for epilepsy (Fig. 48). The two hemispheres are connected by bundles of axons whose function is to relay information back and forth between the two hemispheres. Without this cross-flow of information it is impossible for the two hemispheres to work together. It is as if two pianists were attempting to play a piano duet without being able to hear one another. Following surgery a patient, in effect, has within his skull two brains operating independently. The disconnection of the two hemispheres, which is termed a **split-brain operation**, is drastic surgery and is only

---

Figure 48 Split-brain operations. A top view of the brain shows the interconnecting axons that are severed in split-brain operations. In the lower part of the illustration, a split-brain man tests the verbal ability of his nondominant (right) hemisphere. In the test a picture of a spoon is flashed to the right hemisphere; with his left hand the subject examines various hidden objects by touch, seeking the spoon. The right hemisphere can perform the task correctly but cannot verbalize what the object is.

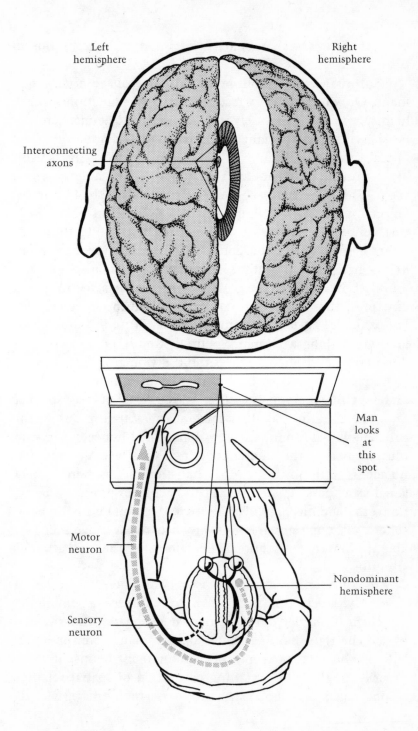

Left
hemisphere

Right
hemisphere

Interconnecting
axons

Man
looks
at
this
spot

Motor
neuron

Nondominant
hemisphere

Sensory
neuron

done in rare cases of epilepsy resistant to other forms of treatment.

Surprisingly, the split-brain patients behave almost normally. Only in laboratory tests do the special functions of each hemisphere show themselves. The dominant hemisphere can be shown to be specialized for language, computation, and logical thinking. When a split-brain patient speaks he is using his dominant hemisphere. The nondominant hemisphere is silent. This mute hemisphere deals with music, the location of objects in space, and other nonverbal tasks. Tests have shown that split-brain patients can direct behavior and "think" in either hemisphere. Thus, consciousness is not a feature of one hemisphere over the other. Although both hemispheres can "think," they do not necessarily carry out the same functions or express the results of their "thought" in the same manner. For example, an embarrassing stimulus (a nude human) was presented, along with many neutral stimuli, only to the nondominant hemisphere. The patient, a woman, reacted to the embarrassing stimulus by blushing, squirming in her chair, and laughing nervously. When asked what it was she had seen, she could not identify the embarrassing stimulus. In this case the verbal, dominant hemisphere had not seen the stimulus, and since the interconnecting axons were severed, had no access to the information. The verbal hemisphere, in fact, acted as a "passive" observer of the behavior produced by the nonverbal hemisphere. For its part the nondominant hemisphere, although not able to "verbalize" what it had seen, was able to produce emotional reactions to the embarrassing stimulus.

In another situation the two hemispheres were simultaneously given the same task to perform—assembling a geometrical puzzle. The dominant hemisphere primarily controlled the right hand, and the nondominant hemisphere the left. As you might expect, the nondominant hemisphere was superior in this task entailing perception of spatial relations among objects. When instructed to assemble the puzzle, the dominant hemisphere tried to do so. The total result was that the nondominant hemisphere's hand would make good progress on the task only to have the dominant hemisphere's hand mess it up. The two hemispheres were in conflict to the extent that the left hand would actually try to restrain the right hand. Such conflict is not seen in the normal brain in which the two hemispheres communicate with each other to produce integrated behavior. As we have seen, the split-brain person is deprived of this ability. As a result the two hemispheres can be taught or can develop incompatible responses to a single stimulus, resulting in conflict between the behavioral responses called for by the two "brains." The split-brain patients, although few in number, have shown us that the functions of the two hemispheres are separate. Each hemisphere is capable of complex mental operations. Such patients may be said to quite literally possess two brains or even two separate "consciousnesses."

Our awareness of the world about us is in a continual state of flux. We drift from being alert and attentive to being bored and disinterested, with alarming speed. In fact, some states of awareness—such as sleeping—are characterized by very little "awareness" of the external world. Yet while sleeping we experience very vivid impressions of an external world not really there. Such periods of dreaming take place in an altered state of awareness. Few would deny the *apparent* reality of a vivid dream. Yet all of us (except small children) recognize that the dream was unreal—that it occurred in an altered state of awareness.

The state of awareness of man and animal is continually being altered by events within and around them. Any stimulus that acts on an organism is either meaningful or not. A meaningful stimulus will alter an organism—if only briefly. The state of awareness of an organism is thus continually being altered by meaningful stimuli. The influences on our awareness are many and of varying strengths. The annoying buzzing of a fly and the powerful influence of lack of sleep are unequal modulators of states of awareness. Some of these altered states of awareness have profound effects on the brain as we have seen in our discussion of the EEG and sleep (pages 106–111).

Drugs are powerful awareness-altering agents. Their power to alter brain function comes from the fact that many of them mimic or oppose such chemical reactions as synaptic transmission in the brain. Other drugs enhance or depress activity in certain areas of the brain in order to produce their effect. Although there exist many ways to alter awareness (education, music, sports, travel, conversation), drugs remain as perhaps the most popular agents. In part this is due to the intensity of their effect and in part to their fast action.

Drugs and Behavior

We are a nation of pill takers. Taking drugs has both beneficial and detrimental effects, but most of us would agree that the beneficial far outweigh the detrimental. Nevertheless, some drugs are consumed for decidedly nonmedical reasons. The history of man is well documented regarding drugs that were used in former times, often as a part of religious pursuits, to induce altered states of awareness. But never before have such a variety of drugs existed that have the power to change behavior or the experience of living. Table 5 gives the major categories of "psychoactive" drugs and their effects.

Narcotic drugs. These drugs have been known for centuries as powerful agents for relieving pain and producing a marked sense of well-being. These drugs, for example, *morphine and heroin*, are the most addictive agents known to man. Addiction is not completely understood but involves a powerful biological need for the substance. If drugs are withheld from an addict, he suffers withdrawal symptoms, which range in severity but are all acutely unpleasant; withdrawal effects can even be fatal. The most potently addicting drugs are also those whose withdrawal effects are most severe.

Table 5 Psychoactive drugs

Type	Examples	Effect
Narcotic	Morphine Heroin	Relieve pain, promote feelings of well-being; addictive
Stimulant	Caffeine Nicotine Amphetamines	Relieve fatigue, increase awareness, decrease appetite; produce anxiety; moderately addictive
Psychogenic	LSD Mescaline Psilosibin Marijuana	Produce psychosis-like states; hallucinations; distortions of space and time; nonaddictive
Alcohol	Whiskey	Stimulate appetite; produce euphoria; impair perceptions; may damage brain and liver of long-term users; potentially addictive
Psychotherapeutic	Antipsychotics reserpine chlorpromazine	Reduce psychotic behavior
	Antianxiety drugs meprobamate chlordiazepoxide	Act as tranquilizers
	Antidepressants imipramine	Reduce depression; other effects similar to those of the stimulants

In contrast to these biologically addicting drugs are the psychologically "addicting" drugs such as *marijuana*. These are not addicting in the physiological sense of the word. A regular marijuana user experiences no physiological symptoms if his pattern of use is broken. He continues to use the drug because he likes it.

Stimulant drugs. Some of the most common drugs used in the United States are the stimulants. The mild forms include *caffeine*, which is in coffee, tea, and cola, and *nicotine*, which is in tobacco. These mild stimulants act to excite the brain, alleviate fatigue, and serve as a general "pick-me-up." They are rather safe and have no side effects for most people. (It is not the nicotine in cigarettes that causes cancer; other agents present in burning tobacco are carcinogenic.)

The most abused of the stimulants are the *amphetamines*. These are powerful agents used to alleviate fatigue, increase awareness, decrease appetite, and reduce the need for sleep. They produce euphoria (a feeling of elation . . . a "high"), often followed by depression. These drugs have been abused. Continued overuse of amphetàmines results in a condition similar to psychosis (a defective or lost contact with reality). The drugs are addicting. Their medical uses are in combatting abnormal drowsiness and serving as an aid to weight loss.

Psychogenic drugs. These drugs are capable of creating psychosis-like states. Members of this group include *LSD, mescaline, psilosibin*, and *marijuana*. Many of these drugs have been around for centuries. In fact at one time marijuana was prescribed by American physicians for the relief of certain conditions. The drugs produce hallucinations (visions of objects that are not present), euphoria, and psychosis-like behavior.

LSD and its derivatives are the most powerful and dangerous drugs in this group. They have powerful and peculiar distorting effects on sensory experience. The resulting behavior can also be bizarre. Many persons have been hospitalized as the result of an unpleasant LSD experience. Many others have reported that symptoms felt while under the effect of LSD spontaneously recur later.

Marijuana is a mild psychogenic drug with few side effects. Its main effect is to produce a mild state of euphoria. It exists in a concentrated form as *hashish*, which is nearly as powerful as LSD. Marijuana, like the other psychogenic drugs, is not addictive.

Alcohol. The drug that has the most widespread use and the greatest cultural acceptance in the United States is *alcohol*.

In small amounts, alcohol appears to stimulate the appetite and produce a mild euphoria, and has few side effects, although it is actually a depressant drug. In greater amounts or when taken by chronic alcoholics the situation is altogether different. There are distortions of time and space, lack of co-ordination, impaired perception, and liver and brain damage. Alcohol is considered to be responsible for a large share of the annual tens of thousands of highway fatalities. It must be considered a dangerous and potentially addicting drug when consumed in large amounts.

Psychotherapeutic drugs. The era of the insane asylum is gone, partly because of an awakening of humanity in man but partly because of a revolution in drug technology. No drug can cure mental illness. The action psychotherapeutic drugs is like that of the aspirin—offering symptomatic relief. That they do not cure mental illness does not mean that medicine has achieved a false victory. Indeed aspirin makes tolerable a splitting headache and allows the person to function in a near-normal manner. So it is with these drugs.

The psychotherapeutics are of three varieties. The *antipsychotics* reduce the severity and duration of psychotic behavior. The mechanism of action is unknown (as indeed it is for many drugs—including aspirin). The *antianxiety* drugs, or tranquilizers, produce an effect similar to mild doses of alcohol but without the sleep-producing effects. These drugs are prescribed when it is desirable to reduce anxiety and produce some euphoria. The last variety of psychotherapeutic drug is the *antidepressant*. These drugs are used in cases of depression (undue sadness with no cause). Their effect is similar to that of the amphetamines but longer lasting.

In using any drug, whether it be for sport or on doctor's orders, the prudent person should recall that these are chemicals foreign to the body and should exercise caution in their use. Drugs are the result of wonderful scientific advances but should not be misused or abused.

The sum total of all of our brain processes operating together determines consciousness. Brain scientists are only now beginning to understand the brain mechanisms that underlie consciousness. Split-brain operations have shown quite dramatically that there is a considerable division of labor between the hemispheres of the normal human brain. The dominant hemisphere is specialized for language, computation, and logical thinking. The nondominant hemisphere is mute and responsible for the location of objects in space. Normally, however, the two hemispheres communicate with each other to produce an integrated output. Following surgical disconnection of the two hemispheres, however, it is possible to see the specialization of each.

Our awareness of the world around us is in continual flux. We fluctuate from wakefulness to sleep, from arousal to lethargy. Some of the more potent external modulators of awareness are the drugs that act upon the brain. There are narcotic drugs, stimulants, psychogenic drugs, alcohol, and psychotherapeutic drugs. Like most advances in science, drugs are both very beneficial and potentially harmful.

The brain may be the most complex thing in the universe. Its operation is certainly more complicated than the most intricate computer. The behaviors that it produces are infinite in their variety. The brain sciences have only begun to explain the functioning of the brain. We may never get to the point where we "understand" completely its operation. Men and women have been trying to understand our species and its situation for centuries. Judging by our present condition, beset with war and violence, poverty and prejudice, and pollution and exploitation, these efforts have not succeeded. If the brain sciences can provide any understanding at all of man, then the effort is decidedly worthwhile.

It is hoped that the reader of this little book has gained some appreciation of his own nervous system and of the fact that all that he or she is and does is the result of brain activity. If so, then the book has succeeded in its mission.

SUGGESTIONS FOR FURTHER READING

Barron, F., Jarvik, M. E., and Bunnell, S., Jr. The Hallucinogenic Drugs, *Scientific American*, April 1964. (Offprint 484)

Brazier, M. A. B. The Analysis of Brain Waves, *Scientific American*, June 1962.

Gazzaniga, M. S. The Split Brain in Man, *Scientific American*, August 1966. (Offprint 508)

Grinspoon, L. Marihuana, *Scientific American*, December 1969. (Offprint 524)

Hall, C. S. What People Dream About, *Scientific American*, May 1951.

Harlow, H. F. Love in Infant Monkeys, *Scientific American*, June 1959. (Offprint 429)

Harlow, H. F., and Harlow, M. K. Social Deprivation in Monkeys, *Scientific American*, November 1962. (Offprint 473)

Jouvet, M. The States of Sleep, *Scientific American*, February 1967. (Offprint 504)

Kimura, D. The Asymmetry of the Human Brain, *Scientific American*, March 1973. (Offprint 554)

Kleitman, N. Patterns of Dreaming, *Scientific American*, November 1960. (Offprint 460)

Kohler, I. Experiments with Goggles, *Scientific American*, May 1962. (Offprint 465)

Olds, J. Pleasure Centers in the Brain, *Scientific American*, October 1956. (Offprint 30)

Sperry, R. W. The Great Cerebral Commissure, *Scientific American*, January 1964. (Offprint 174)

Sperry, R. W. Hemisphere Deconnection and Unity in Conscious Awareness, *American Psychology* 23 (1968):723–733.

Teyler, T. J. *Altered States of Awareness.* San Francisco: W. H. Freeman and Company, 1972.

von Holst, E. and von Saint Paul, U., Electrically Controlled Behavior, *Scientific American*, March 1962. (Offprint 464)

GLOSSARY

action potential: the nerve impulse, a transient alteration of the neural membrane that allows a brief flow of ions. The action potential travels down an axon and can be measured electrically.

adaptation: the tendency of a sensory neuron to cease responding to a nonchanging stimulus.

affective categories: categories into which a person places objects or experiences according to his positive or negative reactions.

alpha activity: brain activity of a particular frequency associated with relaxed wakefulness.

androgen: a male gonadal hormone.

association cortex: a portion of the cortex concerned with complex processes such as the manipulation of symbolic elements.

aphasia: a disturbance of language. There are many forms of it such as difficulties in speaking, reading, or understanding.

auditory canal: the external ear canal leading to the eardrum.

autonomic nervous system: the portion of the nervous system that regulates physiological functions not normally under conscious control—such as heart rate and blood pressure.

axon: a process of a neuron, often quite long, that can release chemical transmitters from its end to affect an adjoining neuron or muscle.

basilar membrane: a stiff membrane in the cochlea upon which are found the hair cells of the inner ear.

behavioral plasticity: modifiability of behavior as the result of experience (e.g., through classical conditioning or habituation). It does not refer to unlearned changes provoked by such factors as fatigue.

biofeedback: information communicated to a human or an animal by artificial means about one of its physiological responses (e.g., heart rate) in order that the subject may attempt to modify the response.

brainstem: a collection of neural structures located at the base of the brain closely associated with the autonomic nervous system.

cell body: enlarged region of a neuron that contains the nucleus.

central nervous system: the brain and spinal cord.

cerebellum: a neural center for the coordination of movement.

chemical senses: the sensory systems concerned with smell and taste. They respond to molecules suspended in air or liquid.

classical conditioning: the establishment of a new response to a neutral stimulus after repeated associations with a meaningful stimulus.

cloning: production of new organisms without sexual reproduction. Under certain conditions DNA transplanted from a cell of one organism into an egg cell of another organism will direct the "construction" of an organism identical to the donor.

cochlea: the structure in the inner ear containing the sound-transducing hair cells.

conditioned response: the learned response to a neutral stimulus in classical conditioning.

cones: photoreceptor neurons of the retina that operate in daylight and convey color information.

contact comfort: the force that binds an infant monkey to a mother monkey.

control: elimination of the effects of extraneous variables on a phenomenon.

cornea: the transparent tissue through which light is crudely focused onto the retina of the eye. The lens performs the final, precise focusing.

cortex: a layer of neurons on the surface of the brain of man and higher organisms.

dendrite: a many branched process of a neuron that conveys information to the cell body. A dendrite may be associated with many synapses.

diabetes: a disease characterized by insufficient amounts of insulin in the blood leading to tissue starvation.

electroencephalogram (EEG): a graphic record of the brain's electrical activity measured through the scalp.

endocrine gland: a gland that releases a hormone into the blood.

estrogen: a female gonadal hormone.

estrous cycle: cyclic changes in gonadal hormone levels and behavior.

ethologist: a scientist who is primarily concerned with the study of animal behavior.

experimental control group: a group of subjects maintained throughout an experiment without special treatment to provide a basis against which the behavior of other groups can be evaluated.

extrapyramidal system: one of two systems for transmittal of motor output from the brain.

field method: the observation of phenomenon in its natural setting.

forebrain: the largest subdivision of the brain of man. It comprises the cortex, thalamus, hypothalamus, pituitary, and limbic system. It is the phylogenetically most recent brain structure.

fovea: a small area of the retina containing tightly packed cones. The fovea is used in looking directly at an object.

frontal lobe: a division of the cortex, site of cortical motor areas.

gonadotrophic hormone: a hormone released by the pituitary gland causing an increase in activity of the gonads.

habituation: the reduction of a response to an unchanging stimulus that is repeatedly presented.

homeostasis: maintenance of conditions in the body within a narrow range by a collection of mechanisms including hunger, thirst, activity, temperature-regulating mechanisms and so forth.

homunculus: the receptortopic representations of the body on the motor and somatic sensory areas of the cortex. Each representation is that of a disproportioned figure.

hormone: the chemical product of an endocrine gland.

hypothalamus: a tiny portion of the brain concerned with the regulation of eating, drinking, temperature, and other functions.

innate behavior sequence: a complex sequence of behaviors that appears to the human observer to be purposeful. It is elicited by a specific stimulus and primarily under genetic influence.

instrumental learning: a method of altering behavior in which the response to be established is reinforced when it appears.

interneurons: neurons specialized to integrate information from other neurons and to activate appropriate response patterns. The bulk of the brain of man is composed of interneurons.

kinesthetic sense: the sensory system concerned with the orientation and location of the different parts of the body.

laboratory method: the examination of a phenomenon in an environment in which the variables are controlled.

limbic system: a collection of many neural structures involved with emotionality, motivation, and perhaps aggression and memory.

manipulation of symbolic elements: complex human behaviors entailing the use of abstract symbols (such as language).

meninges: the membranes covering the brain.

motor neurons: neurons specialized to direct the action of the body's musculature.

myofibrils: the contractile portion of the muscle. Each muscle has millions of the myofibrils. During contraction the proteins in the myofibrils slide past one another, shortening the muscle.

nerve: a bundle of neural processes found outside the brain, usually axons.

neuron: a nerve cell (or brain cell). Neurons are specialized for communication and integration.

occipital lobe: a division of the cortex, site of cortical visual areas.

olfactory bulb: an extension of the brain concerned with the sense of smell.

ossicles: three tiny bones linking the eardrum with the cochlea.

parasympathetic division: the portion of the autonomic nervous system that operates to conserve and maintain bodily resources.

parietal lobe: a division of the cortex, site of cortical body sense areas.

peripheral nervous system: the network of nerves and receptors lying outside of the brain and spinal cord. It comprises the autonomic nervous system and the somatic nervous system.

photochemicals: chemicals in the rods and cones whose molecular configurations are altered upon exposure to light.

pinna: the portion of the ear visible to the eye. Its function is to direct sound waves into the ear.

pituitary: the master gland. Works closely with the hypothalamus to regulate such functions as reproductive cycles, tissue growth, temperature, and water balance.

progesterone: a female gonadal hormone.

pyramidal system: one of two systems for transmittal of motor output from the brain.

REM sleep: rapid eye movement sleep, associated with periods of EEG activation and dreaming.

receptortopic: representative of a receptor surface. For example, the body surface is represented on the parietal lobe of the cortex.

reductionist: a person who seeks to explain a phenomenon by reducing it to the parts of which it is constituted.

reflex: a protective reaction of an organism to a potentially harmful stimulus.

reinforcer: a stimulus used in instrumental learning that tends to increase the probability of repetition of the response preceding it (e.g., food, praise). A reinforcer can also be negative (e.g., electric shock, criticism), in which case the probability of repetition of the preceding response is decreased.

releaser: a stimulus capable of eliciting an innate behavior sequence.

repeatability: the capability of an experiment to be repeated, in order that the original findings may be verified or invalidated.

reticular formation: a diffuse area of the core of the brain concerned with arousal and alerting.

retina: the light-sensitive portion of the eye.

rods: photoreceptor neurons of the retina that operate under dim illumination and convey only black and white information.

sensitization: an augmentation of a response to a stimulus.

sensory neurons: neurons specialized to transduce sensory stimuli (light, sound, pressure) into neural potentials.

somatic nervous system: a subdivision of the peripheral nervous system concerned with relaying movement commands to muscle and relaying sensory information from receptor to brain.

somatic sensory system: the sensory system concerned with sensations at the body surface such as touch and temperature.

spinal cord: an extension of the central nervous system that contains motor neurons which supply the trunk and limb muscles. It is encased in the vertebrae.

split-brain operation: the surgical disconnection of the two hemispheres.

sympathetic division: the portion of the autonomic nervous system that operates to mobilize bodily resources for action.

synapse: the gap between the axon of one neuron and the dendrite or cell body of another. The transmitter chemical from the axon is released into the synapse where it affects the second neuron.

taste buds: specialized structures for taste located primarily on the tongue.

taxis: a movement toward or away from a stimulus.

tectorial membrane: a stiff membrane opposite the basilar membrane of the cochlea. Sensory hair cells are stimulated by vibrations that cause them to rub against this membrane.

temporal lobe: a division of the cortex, site of cortical auditory areas.

thalamus: a sensory relay area in the brain that is also concerned with arousal and attention.

transmitter: the chemical released from an axon that influences an adjoining neuron or muscle. Transmitters can be excitatory or inhibitory.

variables: changing facets of a phenomenon brought about by effects of the environment or an organism's heredity.

vasectomy: the surgical removal of a part of the vas deferens (the structure that carries sperm).

vertebrae: the bony skeleton encasing the spinal cord.

visual cliff: a device for testing an organism's fear of depth.

INDEX